M⬤CK

RETIREMENT

HOW PRACTICING RETIREMENT MAKES FOR A PERFECT RETIREMENT

PETER DUNN

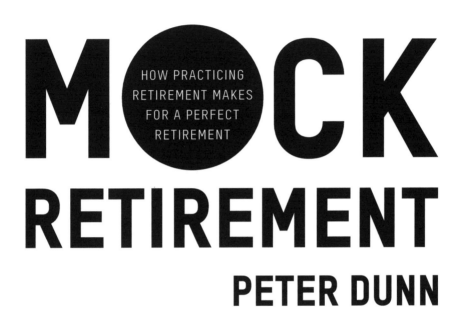

M●CK

HOW PRACTICING
RETIREMENT MAKES
FOR A PERFECT
RETIREMENT

RETIREMENT

PETER DUNN

© 2013 All rights reserved.

978-0-9834588-3-8 Mock Retirement

Library of Congress Control Number: 2013945136

Interior and Cover Design: Lindsay Hadley

Dedication.

To my mom. Your unwavering
love and support inspire me daily.
—*Pete*

Table of Contents

RETIREMENT, OR FINANCIAL INDEPENDENCE AS IT'S OFTEN CALLED, REQUIRES PRACTICE.

But until this book, there hasn't been a method that allows a person to practice being retired. *Mock Retirement* provides the perfect set of exercises that will allow you to retire correctly, mainly because you will practice living on your retirement income. At first thought, retirement doesn't seem as though it would require practice. For years, investment professionals and financial planners have emphasized to you the importance of a retirement plan, but no one has told you that you need to practice being retired. Well, you need to practice being retired. During retirement, passive and investment income need to support your current expenses, forever.

The forever part is where most people slip up. Although your repeatable income is important in retirement, it's your lifestyle and spending habits which will dictate the viability of your retirement plan.

This book isn't about investing or choosing the right investments for your retirement. However, it is the perfect compliment to the conversations you have with your financial advisor. It's quite possible your financial advisor gave you this book. Most financial advisors attack retirement from an investment planning perspective, as they should. Your advisor should be an expert in helping you pick the investments that support your financial goals. This book will actually help you develop and understand your goals. In addition, this book will help you thoroughly examine the spending that takes place to support these goals in retirement.

Although many people don't even have concrete retirement goals, it somehow doesn't stop them from doubting their ability to retire. The statistics are shocking. Eighty percent of people believe they won't be able to put enough money away for retirement. That's a very scary number, yet the number tells us nothing. Your ability to accumulate enough assets to retire is beyond vital. But it isn't the only ingredient in the recipe for success. You must master, yes master, budgeting to ensure a successful retirement. I realize this scenario doesn't sound very appealing. Budgeting has an amazing track record, but it doesn't seem very fun or relaxing. If you find budgeting to be tedious and "not for you," then you're doing it wrong. Budgeting is as tolerable as it is practical.

It may seem at first glance as though this book is for pre-retirees, meaning people in their 40s, 50s, and 60s. It is, but my definition of pre-retirees is a bit different. We are all pre-retirees. And if you are already retired, yet you are doing it wrong, this book could save you from the bitterest of ends: outliving your money. No matter your age or stage in life, this book is relevant. Your future is in this book. In fact, many of the assertions made in this book regarding the absence of pensions and the exit of Social Security retirement become a bigger problem for you the younger you are. In many ways, the eventual retirement of today's 20 year olds is more frightening than the imminent retirement of today's 55 year olds. Whereas the absence of a pension may prove challenging for 55 year olds, the likely single retirement income source that will be available for 20 year olds is daunting.

If you are reading this as a person more than 15 years or so from retirement, you're in luck. Being cognizant of what retirement planning is really about will serve you well. Not only will you have more time to accumulate retirement assets, but you also will have more time to lessen your dependency on your current income. No matter your age, we've already come to one of the most important concepts in your financial life, and we're not even to the first real chapter of the book yet. You should make a concerted effort not to spend all of your income, not because you need to save it, although you do, but because you won't become dependent on the income's existence. It's a shockingly simple concept. The national savings rate, the percentage of money saved by Americans every year, suggests Americans have spent between 98.4% and 94.2% of their incomes over the last twenty years. Ignoring the lack of accumulation going on this period, which in itself is terrifying, how in the world is someone supposed to retire when he or she hasn't shown any propensity for fiscal restraint? You're right, he or she won't be able to. Have you ever considered the idea that retirement is challenging not because of the income available, but instead because of the dependency on a previous income, a working income?

This book isn't one giant rhetorical question. Although I certainly want you to think hard about the concepts posed, you need to take action. Plenty of questions will be met with plenty of answers. And as over-the-top as it might sound, if this book can't solve your retirement problem, then it can't be solved. You are going to learn how to control everything you can possibly control in the retirement planning process. Yet, there are things you won't be able to control. For instance, the more risk you take with your investments, the less control you will have over the amount of money you retire with. This isn't to dissuade you from taking risk, however. We will discuss risk and common misunderstandings of risk in *Chapter 3*.

AS YOU MAKE YOUR WAY THROUGH THIS BOOK, I HOPE YOU QUICKLY REALIZE RETIRE-MENT PLANNING HAS VERY LITTLE TO DO WITH LUCK.

Having spent nearly 15 years assisting people with retirement planning, I can tell you a "we'll see what happens" attitude is quite prevalent in the minds of pre-retirees. Admittedly, pre-retirees will never completely know what their investments will do prior to retirement. Unfortunately, this investment uncertainty has clouded the overall confidence in our ability to impact our financial future. This is both empowering and slightly ominous. *You* are in charge. *You* will decide whether or not your retirement plan works. *Luck* is a bit player. *You* are the star.

CHAPTER ONE

LOOKING BACK
TO LOOK FORWARD

WE ARE BOTH BLESSED AND CURSED BY OUR PAST. OUR PAST SETS OUR EXPECTATIONS, WHETHER THE EXPECTATIONS ARE REALISTIC OR RIDICULOUS.

For instance, we complain about the high price of gas because our initial frame of reference for the price of fuel was significantly less than what we pay for it now. This isn't good or bad, it's just our reality. What we see and what we learn are what we are left to work with. There's one image most of us have had in our minds for decades: our grandparents' retirement lifestyle. At first, our memories of their retirement seem inconsequential, but inconsequential they're not. The view of our own future retirement is tainted, yes tainted, by our view of our ancestors' retirement.

A great deal has changed since our grandparents retired. For starters, corporate America has changed. Corporate America has changed the way it does business, but more importantly, corporate America has changed the way it compensates its workers. This is significant. Your understanding of how compensation structures have changed will go a long way in determining the comfort level of your retirement. That statement seems dramatic, but I assure you it's not. Let's go ahead and list the concepts you need to be comfortable with in order to have a successful retirement.

1. An understanding of how corporate America's compensation structures have changed.

2. An understanding of the four pitfalls that ruin most retirement plans in the 21st century.

3. An understanding of how debt can prevent retirement.

4. An understanding of your income sources in retirement.

5. An understanding of the role budgeting should play in retirement.

Technically, you could probably stop reading this book right now, but in order to master these concepts and to understand how they truly affect you, you should probably keep reading.

Money is never about math. Ever. In fact, proper money management has nothing to do with math. Think about the biggest financial challenges you have ever faced. Take yourself back to that time. What was the challenge? How did it make you feel? How did you overcome the challenge? Whatever the problem, its effect, and its solution, math had nothing to do with it. You didn't get into financial trouble because you were bad at math. Your situation didn't wreak havoc on your life because you didn't know math. And you didn't solve the problem because someone finally taught you math. Yet most retirement planning, and any financial planning for that matter, focuses on math. You are told if you save X amount dollars for Y amount of years and earn Z amount of interest, then you'll be able to retire. But does that change your behavior? Generally, it doesn't. You know 2 + 2 = 4, yet this knowledge probably hasn't produced copious amounts of wealth and financial success for you. If you have wealth and economic resources it's because you had a solid financial strategy and remarkable discipline. If you don't have tremendous wealth and economic resources, then you will need a great retirement strategy and amazing discipline. Yes, an old dog will need to learn some new tricks. And no, I didn't just call you a dog. Well, kinda.

Have you ever gone out to dinner with someone terrible at ordering? He indecisively gives the server a complicated order and then changes his mind about what he ordered. How does the experience usually turnout for him? Correct, poorly. The order is often wrong, his expectations are convoluted, and his satisfaction is lacking. Why? Because he didn't know what he really wanted. People who know what they want get the most out of life because they don't waste time with uncertainty in the moments where action is warranted. How can you get what you want, if you don't know what you want? It's a pretty simple question. The clearer you can be about what you want, the easier it will be to get there. The clearer you can be about what retirement needs to look like for you, the more likely you are to be satisfied.

THINGS CHANGE.
RETIREMENT HAS.

My grandfather retired from General Motors. My earliest memories of the concept of retirement come from his retirement. He stopped working and collected a pension check each month from GM. He got bored. He went back to work. He worked for another twenty-plus years. He didn't do anything wrong; however, his life may have been easier had he better defined what retirement meant to him.

Technically speaking, retirement means "to go away." Whether you want to go away or not, you'll probably want to start framing that stage of your life a little differently than "going away." For a time, financial independence was the popular term for what we commonly think of as retirement. Financial independence was used to describe your independence from your earned income. What it failed to note was during retirement you are still very dependent on a pension, Social Security, and/or passive income off your investments. In fact, there isn't much that's independent about financial independence.

You shouldn't be overly concerned about what you call this time in your life, but you should be cognizant of what your preconceived notions of retirement may cause you to do...or not do. Your grandparents and parents may very well have had a pension. While a pension doesn't necessarily guarantee a comfortable retirement, it certainly does provide a stream of income most similar to the income of the retiree, pre-retirement.

You need to distance yourself from the memories of your parents' and grandparents' retirement. The game has changed, and your inability or unwillingness to acknowledge this fact could be your financial downfall.

WHAT DOES RETIREMENT MEAN TO YOU?

This question isn't about golf or fishing. Every retirement discussion inevitably comes down to golf or fishing. Are you going to spend your retirement fishing? Or are you going to spend your retirement playing golf? While focusing on how you are going to spend your time is important, it often distracts people from the heart of the issue: how will your money flow? That's retirement in a nutshell. Your concern and focus should be on one of the most basic economic concepts in the world: how will your money flow? What is going to create income? What is going to use that income? That's it.

There is no doubt you should take some time to visualize your life in retirement. It's an effective and important exercise. Visualization is powerful. Your mind, once given a visual goal, will figure out how to achieve it. This idea goes back to dining out with someone bad at ordering. If you don't really know what you want, how will you measure your satisfaction? You can't. A retirement can and will go wrong if you can't measure its effectiveness.

Your predicted activities and lifestyle in retirement are important because they allow you to plan for costs. While it's great you want to take banjo lessons, it's the cost of the banjo lessons that matters. While it's great you want to travel the country in an RV, it's the cost of this activity that truly affects the rest of your financial life. Throwing caution to the wind and acting on your retirement vision in spite of your financial situation is foolish, but studying your financial situation, and then pursuing your interests accordingly, is wise.

By the end of this book you will know several vital pieces of information.
- You will know approximately what your income will be in retirement.
- You will know approximately what your income should be in retirement.
- You will know what it costs to be retired.
- You will know if you need to work part-time in retirement.
- You will know how much longer you need to work.
- You will have already retired … once.

You see, the entire point of this book is to assess your situation, train you on some new skills, and then practice being retired. You are going to have a mock retirement. Once you learn how much money you will have during your retirement and determine your expenses, then you will reduce your current earned income to that level, and practice living at that level. It's not crazy, it's practice. There are some rules and other ideas you need to know to make this happen, but this will be the most important mock exercise you ever do. Have you ever been part of a building's fire drill? You know, the alarm is sounded at a predetermined time, and then you exit the building in an orderly fashion. If it makes sense to practice fleeing a fire by leaving the building that's on fire, then it makes sense to practice significantly reducing your earned income before the income is reduced, right?

Think of all the random events in your life you rehearsed. At some point you probably rehearsed a dance, despite the fact the dance lasted less than five minutes. You've undoubtedly been to a wedding rehearsal. What does that last? One hour, tops? So why wouldn't you rehearse something you've never done before, yet you are going to do for several decades? And one other thing worth noting: if you retire the wrong way, it threatens the stability of your entire retirement. No pressure, right?

Coming to terms with retirement means finding out if you can financially handle it. You are not necessarily trying to ascertain whether or not you can retire right now. Rather, you are trying to get a feel for your income and expenses at retirement. Sure, you can just jot the numbers down and eyeball it, but you won't get the true experience of what it's like to be retired. You are about to retire for 90 days. This doesn't mean you are going to give up living for the next 90 days, it just means you are going to need to make some tough choices. These are the same choices you will be forced to make in retirement. Shouldn't you practice making those decisions now while you're still working? Yes. Yes, you should.

SELECT YOUR RETIREMENT LIFESTYLE

You have selected the financial lifestyle you are currently living. Whether you like it or not, your financial choices (or those around you) have led you to your current financial lifestyle. Do you want to continue this lifestyle? This isn't a silly exercise. Your answer to this question, and more importantly what your answer means, could have a significant impact on your life.

Consider the possible answers to this question: *Do you want to continue your current financial lifestyle once you retire?*

01
NO, I WANT A BETTER FINANCIAL LIFESTYLE THAN I CURRENTLY HAVE

Oddly enough, this is possible for some people. It's rare, but possible. It's possible for you to increase your financial lifestyle in retirement if you currently are living well below your means. It is also made possible if you have a great deal of money in retirement accounts that aren't accessible until you retire. Another possible situation exists when you are going to activate a pension upon retirement which would pay you more than your final pre-retirement job. This usually happens when the pension is linked to a prior profession, and the final pre-retirement job is unrelated to the pension. Of course, you may also adopt this philosophy if you are being unrealistic. The unrealistic expectation that your retirement lifestyle will outpace your pre-retirement lifestyle is common and troublesome.

02
NO, I WANT A LESSER FINANCIAL LIFESTYLE THAN I CURRENTLY HAVE

This is the path most people should take, but it's not an appealing choice at first glance. More often than not, your final pre-retirement job is the highest paying job you have ever had. And it's not out of the realm of possibility that you may have increased your lifestyle as your income increased over the years. If this is the case, then you will certainly need to reduce your lifestyle when your retirement income begins because your retirement income is likely less than your pre-retirement income.

03
YES, I WANT TO CONTINUE MY CURRENT FINANCIAL LIFESTYLE

This is the most common choice, but that doesn't make it the best choice. In fact, it can be argued it's not a choice at all. People simply continue racking up the same expenses they have always racked up, regardless of how much income they have or whether or not their income is active or passive. Thus, it's not a choice. In a way, it's lazy. It's a travesty to work your entire adult life only to ruin your chance at a successful retirement by being lazy in your last pre-retirement financial choice. If you are going to make this choice, then truly make a choice. Study your pre-retirement income and your retirement income. Study your pre-retirement expenses and your retirement expenses.

THE KEY TO A SUCCESSFUL RETIREMENT

You must attack retirement from both sides of the ledger. You need to establish an intelligent, efficient, and renewable income plan, and you need to lessen your dependence on monthly income. Despite what you might think, the true key to a successful retirement is to reduce your financial obligations. This idea will be discussed at great length in *Chapter 5*. Your willingness to lessen your financial burdens, by eliminating financial obligations, is your best chance to live comfortably in retirement.

The two primary elements of a successful retirement are guaranteed renewable income and efficient household expenses. Most of the retirement planning material available today focuses on creating and planning your guaranteed renewable income. The methods on how to create said income streams are hotly debated. Get ten investment advisors in a room together, and you will likely find ten different methodologies. This book will not focus on your investment choices and vehicles. This book is meant to help you match your income, no matter its source, with the most neglected aspect of retirement planning, your expenses. No nest egg is safe if you spend like a sailor on leave. It doesn't matter if you get 8% or 4% on your retirement assets if you spend 10% of your nest egg every year of retirement.

The most popular discussion point in retirement planning is your retirement income. So this is where we will begin.

CHAPTER TWO

SOCIAL SECURITY, PENSIONS, AND EMPLOYMENT

MOST RETIREMENT INCOME SOURCES CAN FALL UNDER FOUR SIMPLE CATEGORIES: SOCIAL SECURITY RETIREMENT, PENSIONS, PART-TIME EMPLOYMENT INCOME, AND PERSONAL SAVINGS/INVESTMENTS.

You must fully understand how these retirement income sources intersect or don't intersect with your life. You may find you have four out of four of these income streams. Then again, you might find you have only one out of four of these income sources. One thing is certain, no matter how many retirement income streams are available to you, you must know how much money will be available at your target retirement age. As you learn about the retirement income streams below, take your time considering how these will affect your retirement.

SOCIAL SECURITY

Social Security was first established by President Roosevelt in the years before World War II. Originally, it was created as a system of social insurance for citizens, with a focus on unemployment and old age. These days, what is alarming, though, is to understand how the Social Security Administration actually describes Social Security retirement payments. Consider the following quote, found on the Social Security Administration website *(ssa.gov)*.

"Today's Social Security is designed for a few specific purposes: To provide for the material needs of individuals and families; to protect aged and disabled persons against the expenses of illnesses that may otherwise use up their savings; to keep families together; and to give children the chance to grow up healthy and secure."

Uh-oh. Did you pick up on the scary part? Social Security is intended to help protect the savings of the "aged" in the event of illness. Yet over 35% of retirees over the age of 65 rely solely on their Social Security payments for retirement income. They have no savings. Every year, millions of Americans ask Social Security to do a job it was never meant to do: to be the sole source of retirement income.

Social Security is a nice compliment to the rest of your retirement plan, but it shouldn't be the main player in your retirement plan. However, if it happens to be the only source of income for you, your benefits aren't likely to be subject to federal income taxes. If you have additional income sources, you are most likely going to have your social security benefits taxed, to some level.

A thorough discussion of tax ramifications for every retirement income source can be found in the Appendix at the end of the book.

WHEN SHOULD YOU START TAKING SOCIAL SECURITY RETIREMENT PAYMENTS?

There actually is a technical normal retirement age (NRA), according to the Social Security Administration. Your NRA is based on the year you were born. If you were born before 1937, then your NRA is age 65. If you were born after 1960, your NRA is age 67. And if you were born between 1937 and 1960, then your NRA is determined by the table to the right.

While waiting until your NRA will allow you to receive your full retirement benefit, you don't necessarily need to wait until then to take your payments. You can elect to receive payments as early as age 62. If you do take payments prior to your NRA, then you will receive a reduced benefit. For example, if your NRA is 66, and you choose to take payments at age 62, then your benefit will be reduced by about 25%. There's a calculator to help you understand how your early benefit election affects your benefit amount at ssa.gov.

Just because you can take your benefit at age 62 doesn't mean you should take your benefit at age 62. If you take your benefit early and you are still working (and earning income), then your benefit will be reduced even further. There isn't a magic formula for deciding if you should take your benefits early, but if you don't need the money, you are in good health, and you'd like to receive a higher payout at your NRA, then wait until your NRA. If your health is in question, you need the money, and you can't wait until your NRA, then take the early retirement payout.

NORMAL RETIREMENT AGE BY YEAR OF BIRTH	If you were born in ...	Your normal retirement age is ...
	1937 or earlier	65
	1938	65 and 2 months
	1939	65 and 4 months
	1940	65 and 6 months
	1941	65 and 8 months
	1942	65 and 10 months
	1943-1954	66
	1955	66 and 2 months
	1956	66 and 4 months
	1957	66 and 6 months
	1958	66 and 8 months
	1959	66 and 10 months
	1960 or later	67

source SSA.gov

PENSION

According to a *Time* magazine report, in 1980, 39% of private-sector employees had a pension. Yet by 2010, the percentage of people covered by private-sector pensions fell to 15%. That's a drop of 62% in just 30 years. What has caused this shocking drop-off? According to Richard Ippolito and Thomas A. Firey in a 2002 article from *National Review Online*, "[it] was the result of well-intended government action gone awry." Tax changes in 1986 and 1990 caused many pension-based retirement plans to call it quits. Enter, the 401(k) plan.

Since the inception of the 401(k) in 1980, the popularity and use of defined benefit plans, or pensions as they are more commonly known, has fallen. The use of 401(k) plans has grown in inverse proportion to the shrinking of employee pensions. If you happen to have a pension, then you are an increasing minority. Despite the popularity of 401(k)s and their widespread use, the Center for Retirement Research at Boston College reports the median household retirement account balance in 2010 for workers between the ages of 55-64 was just $120,000. In other words, the plans are being offered, but employees aren't fully taking advantage of them.

For those with a pension, choosing your pension distribution option may be one of the most important financial choices you are ever forced to make. There are two main decisions to be made, and neither decision is necessarily easy.

1. Should you take a lump-sum payment in lieu of lifetime monthly pension payments?
2. How should your pension provide for your survivors, in the event of your death?

Before you begin to answer these questions, it's important you take the time to explore how safe your pension is. A pension plan can fail. Some of the biggest companies in the history of the United States have had failed pensions, including United Airlines, Delphi, and Bethlehem Steel. Luckily, there's some good news...and some bad news. The good news is there's a government entity that insures pensions across the United States. It's called the Pension Benefit Guarantee Corporation (PBGC). It steps in when a pension plan goes splat. The bad news is even the PBGC is subject to risk. In 2008, the PBGC's funds, which are used to pay pension obligations, lost 23% of their value when the PBGC decided to change some of its bond holdings into stock holdings. These losses didn't necessarily affect payouts, but they did cause many to question the long-term viability of the PBGC.

As you make your pension election, you should keep the possibility of pension failure in the back of your mind. It can happen. This shouldn't cause you to panic, but if you have a strong reason to doubt the viability of your pension plan, you should thoroughly discuss your options with your financial advisor.

SHOULD YOU TAKE A LUMP-SUM PAYMENT IN LIEU OF LIFETIME MONTHLY PENSION PAYMENTS?

This is a million dollar question. No really, sometimes it is. Of all the conversations you have with your financial advisor, this is among the most important. The question is a question of risk. Are you willing to take on the risk of managing the lump-sum in order to create your retirement income stream? Or are you more comfortable with your former company's ability to manage your retirement income stream?

It's not easy to stare down the barrel of a several hundred thousand dollar lump-sum payment and decide to take a lifetime monthly income stream instead. But sometimes this is the best option.

Let's examine a very simple, yet realistic scenario. You are faced with two options. Option one is to take a lump-sum payment of $800,000. Option two is to take a lifetime payment of $56,000 per year. Which should you choose? You will learn more about retirement distribution rates in the next chapter, but it would take a 7% distribution on your lump-sum to recreate the $56,000 per year retirement income. Do you believe a 7% fixed rate of distribution on your investments to be realistic and/or wise? And what happens if you die? If you choose the annual pension of $56,000, what is your spouse to do when it disappears upon your death? On the other hand, if you take the lump-sum, how should you manage the lump-sum to create a repeatable and reasonable income stream? All of these ideas lead us to the next major question.

HOW SHOULD YOUR PENSION PROVIDE FOR YOUR SURVIVORS, IN THE EVENT OF YOUR DEATH?

If you select the monthly benefit option instead of the lump-sum payment, then you will need to decide how this choice will affect your loved ones, especially your spouse. Most pension plans allow you to elect a smaller monthly benefit in order to provide a portion of the monthly benefit to your spouse, in the event of your death. Can you imagine having a significant amount of your household retirement income ripped away from your spouse when you die? Well, you should imagine it, because if you choose the wrong payout option, then it will be reality.

There are various strategies you can employ to prevent an income meltdown when you die. If you elect a monthly payment from your pension plan, then consider taking a reduced amount of income up front in order to provide an income stream to your spouse. Or better yet, elect to take the highest monthly payment possible, and then ensure your spouse is taken care of by buying the appropriate amount of life insurance to replace the lost benefit upon your death. This strategy allows you to maximize your pension and provide for your spouse. However, there are some additional considerations when employing this strategy, such as insurability and insurance affordability. In addition, if you choose to go this route, make sure you get qualified for life insurance before making your final pension election. And as always, you should certainly discuss this strategy with your financial advisor. Being able to maximize your pension, via the use of life insurance, is a brilliant move with very few risks. You just need to be able to qualify for the life insurance, and you must be able to afford the life insurance premium. Neither of these "ifs" should be taken for granted.

LIFE WITHOUT COLA

Don't worry, I'm not asking you to give up soft drinks. One of the drawbacks to selecting the monthly pension option is you likely won't receive a Cost of Living Adjustment (COLA) as time rolls on.

This means you won't receive a raise. If you start receiving $2,200/month from your pension when you are 62, you will still only receive $2,200/month when you are 82. If you don't have any other retirement income streams, this could be a problem. Yes, we are talking about inflation. Consumer goods and services tend to gradually increase in price over time. If your retirement income sources are primarily fixed in nature, meaning you won't get a COLA, then you risk not being able to afford your exact same life, 20 years from now. Before you make your pension decision, be sure to determine whether or not your pension payment will receive a COLA.

TAKING THE LUMP-SUM

If you do choose to take the lump-sum, then it immediately becomes an investment asset. You now take 100% responsibility for what happens to it. You take 100% of the risk. This isn't to scare you, it's just the truth. We'll have a thorough discussion of how to generate income from your investment assets in the next chapter.

EMPLOYMENT

You wouldn't be alone if you chose to work part-time during retirement. According to a 2012 report on the Transamerica Retirement Survey, "the majority of workers in their fifties and sixties plan to work after they retire, with 52% reporting that they plan to work part-time and about 9% reporting that they plan to work full-time. Fewer than one in five workers (19 percent) do not plan to work after they retire." The reasons why people work during retirement vary. Many people work during retirement for health insurance benefits, although the number of people that fail at this strategy outweigh the successful ones tenfold. As you'll learn in Chapter 6, a poor healthcare strategy is one of the biggest impediments to a successful retirement. Many individuals work during retirement to keep their minds fresh and skills relevant. This reasoning is both legitimate and vital, yet this book isn't the proper forum for that discussion.

From a practical standpoint, employment income at retirement may simply be a necessity. You may need the income as part of your retirement income strategy.

CHALLENGES OF EMPLOYMENT INCOME DURING RETIREMENT

On your quest to create guaranteed renewable income, it's important to understand employment income during retirement is not guaranteed renewable income. As is the nature of most part-time jobs, part-time jobs retirees often take are disposable at best. Whereas these jobs might be important, fulfilling, and income-producing, they aren't always reliable. The realistic unreliability of these part-time jobs can cause serious problems for your retirement income plan. Beyond that, it is unrealistic to think you will physically be able to work the entire duration of your retirement. The one thing that will be able to work forever, if you play your cards right, are your investments.

CHAPTER THREE

A TRIP TO MONTE CARLO

FOR A MOMENT, ASSUME THE ONLY FOOD SOURCE ON THE PLANET IS CHICKEN. YOUR ONLY CHOICES FOR SUSTENANCE ARE EGGS OR THE MEAT OF THE CHICKEN.

Every day you are faced with an elementary decision when your stomach starts to growl: eat eggs or eat chicken. However, you should know there are a finite number of chickens. There are limitless eggs, as long as there are chickens to produce the eggs. Eat too much chicken, and you'll run out of eggs. Do you see the problem?

Your retirement plan isn't very different. The income you create off your assets (savings, 401(k), mutual funds, stocks, bonds, etc.) can only be created when there is an asset to create it. In other words, eggs can only be created when there are chickens around. If you run out of chickens, you run out of food. If you run out of assets, you run out of income.

Without a doubt, one of the most heinous financial mistakes you can make in retirement is spending large chunks of money, more specifically, spending more money than you earn in interest on your assets. If you are spending at a faster rate than your assets are earning, then you will undoubtedly go broke. It's worth noting that going broke is bad during retirement. In order to protect yourself from going broke in retirement due to using your income-producing assets for big purchases, you need to have two types of assets: chunk money and income-producing assets.

Chunk money, which is not a technical term, is money used to fund large expenditures such as a vacation, a car, a home repair, or a large medical bill. The role of chunk money is very basic: to prevent you from accelerating the distribution rates of your income-producing assets. You will undoubtedly have expenditures in retirement which require chunks of money. You must set some money aside to deal with these expenses.

On the other hand, income-producing assets are assets designated not to necessarily grow, but to generate a stream of income in retirement. Ideally, this income is produced without cutting into the asset itself. An investment can stick around forever, risk permitting, if you only live off of the interest or income. Having said that, it's preferable the asset actually grows.

There are several ways in which an investment asset can produce a stream of income.

1. INTEREST

You are probably the most familiar with this type of income. Your savings account generates a small percentage of interest. Certificates of deposit (CDs) produce interest and bonds pay interest. Bond interest may have a huge impact on your retirement planning. Retirement planning uses several types of bonds, including municipal bonds, corporate bonds, and treasury bonds. Your financial advisor will be able to assess the appropriateness of bonds for your particular situation.

2. DIVIDENDS

If you own individual stocks or stock mutual funds, you may receive dividends. In short, dividends are your share of the profit of the companies you own. Because as you know, if you own a stock or stock mutual fund, you own part of a company.

3. ANNUITY PAYMENT/WITHDRAWAL

Annuities are a popular tool for creating guaranteed income in retirement. They typically pay out income via two different methods. Traditionally, an annuity creates income by annuitizing an asset. This means the annuity owner gives up complete rights and control of the asset in order to obtain a guaranteed lifetime income stream from the annuity (insurance) company. More recently, annuity owners have been able to secure a guaranteed income stream from their annuities without surrendering rights to the initial deposit. These types of withdrawals are often called guaranteed withdrawal or guaranteed income riders.

4. RENT

If your retirement plan includes receiving payments from your rental properties, then your retirement income will be subsidized with rent.

5. LIQUIDATION

This means you will need to sell your investments in order to create an income stream. You will be cannibalizing the principal. Does that sound ominous? Good, it is. There's no turning back once you dip into the principal. This is why distribution rates are so important.

HOW MUCH INCOME CAN YOUR ASSETS PROVIDE?

I recently surveyed hundreds of financial advisors with an average of 14 years of industry experience. Collectively, this group agreed that the proper distribution rate at retirement is 4%. Your understanding of this concept is vital to the success of your retirement. In order to help you understand this idea better, we should head to Monte Carlo.

MONTE CARLO SIMULATION

A 2010 study conducted by Allianz Life Insurance Company of North America indicates that 61% of individuals fear running out of money in retirement more than death itself. It's quite a scary thought. What would happen if you ran out of money? How likely are you to run out of money? Both of these questions are important to explore.

It has been my experience that very few people do the formal calculations that would help them understand whether or not they are likely to run out of money during retirement. Why? Because it's terrifying. On top of that, they don't know how to figure it out. Most financial advisors should be able to help you with this calculation, yet nearly two thirds of retirees do not have someone they consider to be their financial advisor (based on a 2011 LIMRA report).

Fortunately, there's a very simple tool for figuring out the probability of running out of money over a set period of time given a set withdraw rate. It's called a Monte Carlo simulation. Sounds like gambling, doesn't it? Well, it's not.

Before you peruse these tables using the Monte Carlo simulation method, you should prepare yourself to see some surprising things. As earlier noted, most seasoned financial advisors prefer an asset distribution rate of 4%. Also earlier noted is that only 33% of pre-retirees have someone they consider to be their financial advisor. Lack of good advice likely results in people distributing too much money from their nest egg as retirement income. The following tables will show the results of taking more than the prescribed 4%. In recent years, even the 4% distribution rate "rule" has been called into question by economists and retirement planning experts due to a sustained low interest rate environment. The lower interest rate environment of the early 2010s has made it more difficult to have certainty in the permanency of taking 4% withdrawals and having your money last long enough.

Shortly, you will see several Monte Carlo simulation tables. Each table represents a different investment style. Each table was created by running over 5000 scenarios using various investment indexes' rates of return dating back to 1926. The percentages indicate the number of successful scenarios, successful meaning the simulation didn't result in running out of money. In other words, these tables are thorough and real. One hundred is the best number because it indicates you have a 100% chance of success.

Here's how you read the table. When examining the first Monte Carlo simulation with a 50% bond, 30% cash, 20% stock allocation, you will see that withdrawing 6.5% of your portfolio's value every year, over 25 years during your retirement, only gives you an 18% chance of not running out of money. That's suggesting you have an 82% chance of failure when trying to make a 6.5% distribution rate last 25 years. Thus, the higher the number in the table, the more likely you will have a successful retirement. You will need to decide what is an acceptable rate of success, and what is an acceptable rate of failure.

***The following information and tables may appear to be complicated and intimidating, but they are not. Take your time as you absorb the Monte Carlo simulation concept to ensure you are making the best decisions for you and your family.

Let's examine this concept even further. If you have $300,000 in retirement assets at the beginning of retirement, a 6.5% distribution rate would provide you with an annual income of $19,500. You would then withdraw 6.5% of the balance the next year, no matter the balance of the portfolio. Here's the problem: if your portfolio doesn't provide at least a 6.5% rate of return on the underlying investments, then you would withdraw more money than the portfolio created that year. This means you'll start eating into the principal balance. Additionally, if your portfolio falls in value, you'll need to withdraw more than 6.5% to produce the same dollar amount of retirement income. But if you simply tried to withdraw 6.5% of your total portfolio value every year for 25 years, then there's still only an 18% chance you'll succeed in doing so. There's an 82% chance you'll run out of money along the way. And this accounts for 5000 different investment performance scenarios that the 50% bond, 30% cash, and 20% stock allocation could create.

As you examine the tables below, match the table which most accurately depicts your investment style as you enter retirement. If you don't know what your investment style is or should be, then we have yet another reason for you to find a great investment advisor.

50% BOND / 30% CASH / 20% STOCK

% of portfolio used per year	10 years	15 years	20 years	25 years	30 years
3.00%	100%	100%	100%	100%	100%
3.50%	100%	100%	100%	100%	97%
4.00%	100%	100%	99%	97%	89%
4.50%	100%	100%	99%	91%	73%
5.00%	100%	100%	95%	77%	50%
5.50%	100%	100%	88%	57%	30%
6.00%	100%	99%	72%	35%	14%
6.50%	100%	95%	55%	18%	6%
7.00%	100%	88%	34%	8%	2%
7.50%	100%	74%	19%	3%	0%
8.00%	100%	57%	8%	0%	0%
8.50%	100%	39%	3%	0%	0%
9.00%	98%	24%	1%	0%	0%

60% STOCK / 40% BOND

% of portfolio used per year	10 years	15 years	20 years	25 years	30 years
3.00%	100%	100%	100%	100%	99%
3.50%	100%	100%	100%	98%	96%
4.00%	100%	100%	99%	96%	92%
4.50%	100%	100%	97%	92%	86%
5.00%	100%	100%	94%	85%	79%
5.50%	100%	98%	90%	79%	69%
6.00%	100%	96%	83%	69%	59%
6.50%	100%	92%	75%	60%	48%
7.00%	100%	87%	65%	52%	41%
7.50%	99%	81%	58%	41%	30%
8.00%	98%	74%	47%	32%	23%
8.50%	96%	66%	38%	24%	18%
9.00%	94%	57%	32%	18%	12%

50% CASH / 25% STOCK / 25% BOND

	10 years	15 years	20 years	25 years	30 years
3.00%	100%	100%	100%	100%	100%
3.50%	100%	100%	100%	100%	97%
4.00%	100%	100%	100%	97%	88%
4.50%	100%	100%	99%	90%	70%
5.00%	100%	100%	96%	73%	48%
5.50%	100%	100%	86%	53%	26%
6.00%	100%	99%	73%	33%	12%
6.50%	100%	96%	52%	17%	5%
7.00%	100%	87%	31%	6%	1%
7.50%	100%	74%	16%	2%	0%
8.00%	100%	55%	7%	0%	0%
8.50%	100%	37%	2%	0%	0%
9.00%	98%	21%	0%	0%	0%

100% STOCK

% of portfolio used per year	10 years	15 years	20 years	25 years	30 years
3.00%	100%	100%	99%	97%	95%
3.50%	100%	100%	97%	94%	91%
4.00%	100%	98%	95%	90%	86%
4.50%	100%	97%	92%	86%	82%
5.00%	100%	95%	88%	82%	76%
5.50%	99%	93%	85%	76%	71%
6.00%	99%	89%	80%	70%	65%
6.50%	98%	86%	74%	64%	58%
7.00%	96%	82%	69%	60%	52%
7.50%	95%	78%	62%	52%	46%
8.00%	94%	73%	56%	47%	40%
8.50%	90%	67%	50%	41%	35%
9.00%	87%	62%	45%	35%	30%

25% BOND / 75% STOCK

	10 years	15 years	20 years	25 years	30 years
3.00%	100%	100%	100%	99%	98%
3.50%	100%	100%	99%	97%	95%
4.00%	100%	100%	98%	94%	91%
4.50%	100%	99%	95%	90%	85%
5.00%	100%	98%	93%	85%	79%
5.50%	100%	96%	88%	78%	69%
6.00%	100%	95%	82%	70%	63%
6.50%	100%	91%	75%	61%	54%
7.00%	99%	87%	69%	55%	46%
7.50%	98%	80%	60%	47%	40%
8.00%	97%	74%	54%	40%	32%
8.50%	95%	68%	46%	33%	25%
9.00%	91%	59%	37%	27%	20%

100% BONDS

% of portfolio used per year	10 years	15 years	20 years	25 years	30 years
3.00%	100%	100%	100%	100%	98%
3.50%	100%	100%	100%	98%	90%
4.00%	100%	100%	99%	92%	76%
4.50%	100%	100%	97%	79%	55%
5.00%	100%	100%	89%	60%	36%
5.50%	100%	99%	75%	41%	20%
6.00%	100%	96%	59%	24%	10%
6.50%	100%	89%	39%	12%	4%
7.00%	100%	77%	25%	6%	1%
7.50%	100%	62%	14%	2%	0%
8.00%	100%	45%	6%	1%	0%
8.50%	98%	30%	2%	0%	0%
9.00%	95%	17%	1%	0%	0%

50% BOND / 50% STOCK

	10 years	15 years	20 years	25 years	30 years
3.00%	100%	100%	100%	100%	99%
3.50%	100%	100%	100%	99%	97%
4.00%	100%	100%	99%	97%	93%
4.50%	100%	100%	98%	93%	86%
5.00%	100%	100%	95%	86%	77%
5.50%	100%	99%	90%	78%	65%
6.00%	100%	97%	84%	68%	55%
6.50%	100%	94%	75%	56%	43%
7.00%	100%	89%	65%	44%	33%
7.50%	100%	81%	54%	34%	24%
8.00%	99%	74%	44%	27%	17%
8.50%	98%	64%	33%	18%	11%
9.00%	95%	55%	24%	12%	7%

100% CASH

% of portfolio used per year	10 years	15 years	20 years	25 years	30 years
3.00%	100%	100%	100%	100%	94%
3.50%	100%	100%	100%	97%	65%
4.00%	100%	100%	100%	75%	19%
4.50%	100%	100%	94%	33%	2%
5.00%	100%	100%	73%	6%	0%
5.50%	100%	100%	33%	0%	0%
6.00%	100%	96%	7%	0%	0%
6.50%	100%	81%	1%	0%	0%
7.00%	100%	47%	0%	0%	0%
7.50%	100%	16%	0%	0%	0%
8.00%	100%	3%	0%	0%	0%
8.50%	100%	0%	0%	0%	0%
9.00%	97%	0%	0%	0%	0%

UNDERSTANDING AND MEASURING RISK

Your retirement income plan must be permanent. You cannot, under any circumstance, employ an income plan that leaves you without income as you get older.

You need a proper understanding of risk to make sure this doesn't happen. On some level, risk is necessary. In addition to its necessity, risk is omnipresent. While you may avoid investment risk, you won't be able to avoid inflation risk, interest rate risk, or liquidity risk. Most people's understanding of risk stops at market risk. Market risk is used to describe the possibility of losing money due to financial market activity. An example would be if you lose money when your favorite stock decreases in price. The risk was the financial markets acted naturally, and then you were exposed to the possibility of loss. When people are described as risk-averse, they are actually market risk-averse. They don't want to expose their money to the possibility of loss due to market activity.

Misjudging market risk is one of the main causes of going broke in retirement. Whether you personally make the misjudgment or your financial advisor makes the misjudgment, if your investments decrease in value, then any income taken on those investments only compounds the problem. This doesn't mean you shouldn't take market risk in retirement, it just means you need to understand truly what is at risk. By the end of this book, you will know exactly how much market risk you need to take. It is wise not to take an ounce of market risk more than necessary to accomplish your retirement goal.

In the previous Monte Carlo simulations, you will notice each table represents a different investment allocation. And in turn, each allocation represents a different risk tolerance. The more equity positions in your portfolio (stocks), the more risk tolerant you are. While you can certainly see which allocations work best, you shouldn't necessarily adopt the corresponding investment allocation for your own investments. You should always consult your investment advisor when making major changes to your asset allocation. If you've been a pretty balanced investor in the past, a switch to 100% stock would be a major shock to the system and could be detrimental to both your short-term and long-term financial health. The tables may make you feel like there is one ideal portfolio construction for retirement success, but that isn't the case. Your risk tolerance is very personal. It's your ability to tolerate market fluctuations in your portfolio without freaking out.

If nothing else, the Monte Carlo simulations on the previous pages will help you understand not only the impact your distribution strategy will have, but also your justified unwillingness to take risk with your money. Want to be in 100% cash? That's fine, but your actions no longer have mysterious results. The results are very clear and very real.

TAKING WHAT YOU WANT VERSUS TAKING WHAT YOU NEED

One of the biggest mistakes you can make is to take distributions based on what you want, rather than on what is reasonably available to maintain consistent income throughout your life. You may ask, "But what if I need more income than my assets, pension, and/or Social Security can provide?" Excellent question. Unfortunately the answer, or better yet the answers, to this question can be bitter pills to swallow.

Here are the possible answers to that question:

- You can't retire.
- You can't retire right now.
- You need to re-evaluate what you "need."
- You need to employ the fourth stream of retirement income: employment.

Not to trivialize your desire for more income, but your retirement will end in disaster if you bleed your assets too quickly. Don't ignore the risks and the Monte Carlo simulations discussed earlier. Hoping things work out is a terrible strategy. This is the exact reason why *Mock Retirement* is so important. As you will learn later, identifying a projected retirement income shortfall must lead to action. You cannot wing it. Blindly forcing out too much income is not the same as driving an extra 50 miles with your fuel light on and hoping for the best. Ignorant perseverance will lead to an irreversible outcome.

WHAT'S YOUR PROJECTED INCOME AT YOUR TARGET RETIREMENT AGE?

You understand the different income sources, now you need to project what will be available for you on your retirement date. Before you do this, though, you will need to project your portfolio's value at your retirement date.

The concept of the calculation works like this: take the current value of your investments, plus any additions you will make over the next few years until retirement, all at a hypothetical rate of return until the day you retire. It's a fairly complicated calculation with several moving pieces. But the most important thing for you to know is you should not overestimate the rate of return which you receive on your investments. I've provided a retirement asset projection calculator for you at PeteThePlanner.com/retirement-calculator.

Once you arrive at a projected investment asset total which corresponds with your retirement age goal, then you will need to go back to the Monte Carlo simulation tables from earlier in this chapter. Find the table which most closely matches your projected investment style/philosophy at retirement. For instance, if you believe your portfolio will consist of 60% stocks and 40% bonds, then find the corresponding Monte Carlo simulation table. Now, choose a distribution rate for your income-producing assets. As discussed earlier in the chapter, many investment professionals feel as though 4% is the best bet. If you'd like to choose a different distribution rate, that's fine. You just need to be comfortable with the consequences of your selection.

YOUR PROCESS MIGHT LOOK LIKE THIS:

1. Determine that your $400,000 portfolio will grow to $600,000 over the next 10 years given a particular rate of return and the proper additions.

2. Select the Monte Carlo simulation table created using a 60% stock and 40% bond allocation, if it is indeed your investment style and mix.

3. Select a distribution rate of 4%.

4. Confirm you are comfortable that a 4% distribution rate has a 92% chance for success over 30 years of distributions.

5. Arrive at $24,000 as your first year investment income at retirement.

Add this together with the Social Security retirement estimates provided to you by the Social Security Administration, any rental income, and your projected pension amount (at your target retirement age). This is your gross (before taxes) retirement income. Your final totals would look like the numbers below.

$24,000 from investments
$20,000 from Social Security retirement
$0 pension
$0 rent

$44,000 TOTAL

Our goal for you now is to prove you can live on a gross income of $44,000 (or whatever your total is) during retirement. Your *Mock Retirement* will begin with this number. But before we get to work, there are some other subjects we need to talk about. The conversation begins with debt.

CHAPTER FOUR

PAYING FOR THE PAST

THERE'S NO DOUBT YOUR ABILITY TO RETIRE COMFORTABLY IS DEPENDENT UPON THE ACTIONS YOU TOOK TWENTY, EVEN THIRTY YEARS PRIOR TO RETIREMENT.

Whereas the money you saved for retirement while in your 30s and 40s is certainly vital, the debts you hold into your 50s and 60s are really going to determine how your retirement goes.

On the surface, debt seems like it's only an issue for young families. There's the family home, the family cars, the vacations, the educations, and several other expenses debt seems justified to be a part of. But what happens when the kids move out? What happens when the last family vacation is taken and the last diploma is earned? Unfortunately in today's America, the empty-nesters that so badly want to focus on their relationship again are often left saddled with extensive amounts of debt—debt of every possible variety. Pre-retirees often face mortgage debt, credit card debt, parent student loans, and various other forms of consumer debt. According to a 2013 Census Bureau study, mortgage debt accounts for 78% of all household debt in America. And in the 55 to 64 age category, Americans carry on average $70,000 in debt, which is a 64% increase since the year 2000. These numbers further suggest the average pre-retiree is dealing with nearly $55,000 in mortgage debt and $15,000 in other consumer debt. These totals will make for an uncomfortable and difficult retirement if not dealt with appropriately.

Debt, in itself, isn't evil. It certainly gets a bad rap for ruining financial lives, but its dangers often go misdiagnosed. Debt is mainly harmful for one simple reason: its obligation of repayment occupies your discretionary income. In other words, it's hard to live life when you are using all of your recurring financial resources (income) to pay for something that is part of your past.

It is in your best interest, no pun intended, to pay off your debt prior to retirement. What debts should you pay off? Ideally, most. It's nearly inexcusable to carry credit card debt into retirement. Student loan debt, in the form of parent plus loans, can drain valuable retirement income. But the biggest debt, which creates the biggest wake, is a mortgage.

Carrying a mortgage deep into retirement puts a tremendous amount of pressure on your retirement income sources. If you are fearful you won't have enough money to retire, then make a concerted effort to pay off your biggest retirement expense, such as your mortgage, thus eliminating the need for a copious amount of retirement income. As you will learn in Chapter 6, a poor housing decision leading into retirement is one of the biggest challenges retirees face today.

THE STRANGE OPPORTUNITY THAT PRE-RETIREMENT DEBT OFFERS

Despite the challenges debt can present to a retirement plan, debt reduction just prior to retirement can create a very strange, yet positive, effect. When you commit to liquidating vast amounts of consumer debt, you almost always reduce your spending down to the essentials.

Once committed to this methodology, the longer your spending is based on necessity, the better chance you have to shape your retirement spending habits. For example, let's say your current net monthly household income is $4,500. Of this income, let's say you have $1,600/month in debt payment obligations. What happens when those debt obligations go away? In a way, it means you need $19,200 ($1,600/month for 12 months) less income every year. Can you imagine if you matched this dip in income need with your retirement date? It would be magical. Okay, maybe not magical, but really smart.

You have this opportunity, if you create this opportunity. For years, you may have been worrying about how your consumer debt would affect your ability to retire. However, your debt can actually help you adjust to your retirement income stream, and in addition, it can actually put you in a better position than those not dealing with consumer debt. The final years leading up to retirement are crucial for so many reasons, but none more so than learning to live on less discretionary income. A structured debt paydown is the perfect way to accomplish this goal, but first we need to look at what type of attitude creates debt.

A CLOSER LOOK AT DEBT, AND PAYING IT DOWN

Every bad habit comes equipped with a healthy dose of denial. Debt is no different. Over the years, I've compiled a mental archive of the different ways people try to rationalize their debt or blame it on someone else. Here are some of the most common:

"My finances were in good shape until I got those unexpected medical bills in the mail."

"I had to take out student loans for my kids because I neglected to save for their college education."

"The TV was on sale. I would have been silly not to buy it at that price."

"My car was out of warranty, and I hate driving a car that isn't under warranty."

"I was throwing money away by renting, so it only made sense to buy."

"Our family hadn't been on a vacation in three years. We couldn't afford it, but hey, I didn't want to look like a cheapskate."

The list goes on. But no matter how good your excuse is, there's no gray area when it comes to debt—you're either in it or you're not. And if you're in it, it can only be tackled through discipline, patience and proper planning. As you begin to think about your debt, remember one thing: a debt, is a debt, is a debt. Don't ignore the "12 months same as cash" debt you accrued when you bought your new couch on the promise of no interest for a year. Don't ignore your student loans, even if they're in deferment. (While deferment does allow you to delay your payments, doing so simply puts off the inevitable.) If you owe money to any company, person or other entity, it counts toward your debt total. Compartmentalizing your debt into arbitrary categories merely detracts from your progress.

While we're only dedicating one chapter to the creation of your debt pay down plan, it could take months or even years to get completely out of debt, depending on the amount of debt you have. Don't be discouraged by the impending hard work, though; this plan will get you on a regular payment schedule, make your financial stress progressively easier to manage, and prepare you for your retirement income.

DEBT PAY DOWN PROCESS

STEP 1:
MAP OUT YOUR DEBT.

Before you figure out how you're going to pay off your debt, you need to figure out what debt you actually have. If you are in a bit of denial over your debts, you may have never actually compiled a comprehensive list. To do this, list all of your debts, from the smallest balance to the largest balance, in the table to the right. Allow yourself as much time as necessary to complete this table—and make sure not to leave out any details. Remember, list every type of debt. This includes credit cards, mortgages, car loans, student loans, personal loans, and even debts that have made their way to collections.

WHOM DO YOU OWE?	AMOUNT OWED	MINIMUM PAYMENT	NEW MONTHLY PAYMENT

DEBT PAY DOWN PROCESS

STEP 2:
BUILD MOMENTUM
WITH SMALL VICTORIES.

Don't make equal payments on each debt;
it's inefficient. Employing this strategy may
have been your problem for years. It's not
unusual for people to pay extra on all their
debts. As you know, your debts have a required
minimum payment. Many people do what
they believe to be a good idea and pay more
than minimum payment on all their debts.
Frustration eventually sets in because it doesn't
appear any progress is being made toward the
goal of being debt free. Instead, you should
start by focusing on paying off your smallest
debt and getting the balance down to zero.

This tactic frees up the money you were putting toward the monthly minimum payment so you can put it toward the next debt, not to mention it also helps you create a sense of financial momentum. You may start out only putting $100/month extra above the minimum payment. But by the end of the debt pay down process, you might actually be putting upwards of $1,000/month toward the next-lowest debt balance. This scenario is possible because you eliminated debts and were able to use former minimum payments to help you pay off the next debt.

If you're wondering why we're focusing on the lowest balance instead of the highest interest rate, it's because we're trying to create momentum and zero balances. So, at this point, try not to concern yourself with the interest rates (even though I know it goes against conventional wisdom).

Creating small victories and zero balances up front is the financial equivalent of losing that first five pounds on a diet. You just need some confirmation that what you're doing really works. As you pay off these balances, you'll begin to accumulate the money you were once putting toward minimum payments each month, allowing you to apply those savings to the next-lowest balance on your list.

DEBT PAY DOWN PROCESS

STEP 3:
COMMIT TO A DEBT-PAYMENT SCHEDULE.

This process is as simple as it gets, assuming you commit to making it part of your routine. The key is to keep chipping away at the debt. Sure, it will take time, but it will also work. Every time you free up money in your budget, apply it to your next-lowest balance.

As a personal finance expert, I'm always tempted to create complicated processes for debt liquidation. But the reality is you need a very simple plan that's easy to stick to. Debt liquidation is way too important to complicate with confusing financial algorithms and impossible goals.

YOUR PERSPECTIVE NEEDS TO SHIFT

There's no doubt your debt is a hinderance. But if you shift your perspective, then this hinderance immediately becomes a legitimate opportunity. This isn't some sort of strange exercise in semantics. Your debt, if you pay it down between now and your retirement date, may actually put you in a better position over those that are spending a vast majority of their pre-retirement income on consumer habits which have been formed for a decade or more. Whereas those people are forcing themselves to quit a learned habit, you are employing brilliant, healthy habits as you head into your retirement.

CHAPTER FIVE

THE HIDDEN KEY TO RETIREMENT

EVERY PERSON IN THE WORLD HAS A LIMITED NUMBER OF FINANCIAL RESOURCES.

Yet, anyone can thrive financially based on how he or she manages these financial resources. A person who mismanages a relatively large amount of assets is going to suffer a predictable fate, whereas an individual who diligently respects a lesser amount of assets has an increased chance to achieve financial longevity. The key component in this equation is budgeting.

Budgeting is a vital part of your retirement planning. Whether you are currently retired or you are a few years from retirement, you not only need to take budgeting seriously, but you also need to make budgeting a priority.

Budgeting is often associated with money; however, you budget the use of resources every single day of your life and don't think twice about it. For instance, you don't eat all of your groceries the moment you get home from the grocery store. You don't clip all the roses off your rose bush at the same time. And most people don't read a 400 page novel in just one sitting. In these examples you budgeted food, flowers, and time. If you have struggled to budget your money in the past, hopefully you can draw some inspiration from your budgeting of other resources.

As a pre-retiree, you must understand the need to develop budgeting skills and habits prior to walking away from your primary job. And as a retiree, you must understand your budget is one of the primary defenses that prevents you from running out of money. Just as you ration your weekly groceries, you must have a structured plan to ration the use of your income.

BUDGETING IS ABOUT HABITS, NOT PENNY-PINCHING

Have you ever convinced yourself you didn't like a particular food, only to find out once you tried it again, you loved it? Many people experience this same phenomenon with budgeting. Tracking your expenses can be tedious, especially if you do it the wrong way. And feeling restricted with your spending can be a negative feeling, if you don't frame it properly.

Before you begin to budget your income, you must understand your propensity to spend money. Some people have formed such harmful spending habits that budgeting, without addressing the poor spending habits, is pointless. Therefore, let's examine your spending habits first. There's no better way to understand harmful spending habits than to learn the story of Daniel and Bonnie.

BONNIE'S TUMULTUOUS TALE OF SPENDING

Bonnie was a stay-at-home grandma. She was a wonderful lady, the type of lady you want to spend an entire afternoon with just talking and drinking iced tea. Her husband, Daniel, was a partner at a local law firm. Daniel made an extraordinarily good living, and he had more than $1,500,000 in a company sponsored retirement plan.

On the surface, Daniel and Bonnie's financial future seemed bright. They lived very comfortably, they traveled often, and Daniel's mid six-figure income could handle almost any spending request. But there was a major-league problem lurking underneath the surface. Not only did they spend every dime they made, but Bonnie also had a wicked spending addiction she didn't know she had. Bonnie and Daniel's spending problems happen to be the two most common byproducts of not having a budget prior to retirement.

1. Over the years, Daniel and Bonnie increased their spending to match their income.
2. Bonnie was addicted to spending money.

Whereas Daniel made several hundred thousand dollars per year while working, in retirement, his projected annual income was closer to $100,000. I know what you are thinking. You're thinking anyone should be able to survive on $100,000 per year in retirement. I don't disagree. However, I ask you to suspend your judgment of their income for just one moment. Let's knock off some zeros. What if Daniel and Bonnie made $50,000 per year right now, and then a projected $10,000 per year in retirement? Would that be a challenge? An 80% reduction of income is challenging, no matter the starting dollar figure. And if bad habits are part of the equation, which in this situation they are, then living on "just" $100,000 per year is actually a monumental task, as silly as it might seem.

Daniel and Bonnie's entire life revolves around Daniel's income. Their monthly mortgage payment is set against it, their lifestyle habits are set against it, and a majority of their financial obligations are set against it. If Daniel were to retire today, then his mortgage payment becomes immediately unaffordable. Your situation may not parallel Daniel and Bonnie's in regard to dollars, but the percentages may be exactly the same. In an instant, Daniel's mortgage payment would go from 15% of his take-home pay to nearly 50% of his retirement income. This is crippling to anyone.

ADJUSTING YOUR SPENDING UP TO MATCH YOUR INCOME

Whether you are preparing for retirement or you are a college kid trying to figure out how money works, allowing your expenses to adjust proportionally to your increasing income is a grave error. The difficulty in decreasing your expenses is the main reason this offense is so deadly. There are several obvious reasons why adjusting your expenses is easier said than done—and there are also some less obvious reasons.

THE OBVIOUS REASONS

1. A mortgage payment based on a large "working" income can be hard to support in retirement. There is a growing trend among pre-retirees in their 50s to purchase a final home once the children have moved out. Unfortunately, this decision usually is based on what the "working" salary can support.

1. Health insurance premiums are ever-increasing. Your "working" income and workplace benefit plans make the premiums reasonably affordable. But what happens when you are responsible for taking over the entire premium if you retire prior to 65?

THE NOT-SO-OBVIOUS

1. Dining habits are hard to break.
2. Financially supporting adult children is hard to stop.

THE IDEAL HOUSEHOLD BUDGET

Your retirement budget will look different than the budget of someone in the middle of his or her career. To the right, you will find the *Ideal Household Budget* for someone not at, or nearing, retirement. Your budget, as a pre-retiree or retiree, should look much different than this.

Does your spending look like the suggested spending to the right? If so, you need to wean yourself from it. As a retiree, your spending shouldn't match the percentages in the Ideal Household Budget, and what's more, you may not have the retirement income to support it. There's an often used nugget in retirement planning which suggests that retirees only spend 80% of what they spent during the last few years prior to retirement. This idea may or may not be true, but there's no way the spending simply disappears. You must examine each and every one of these categories and strategically plan how you intend to reduce your income's commitment to them.

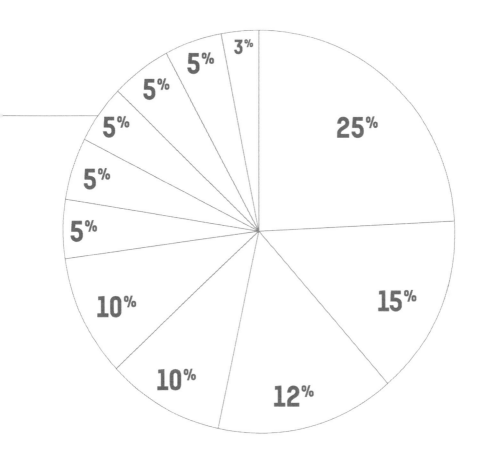

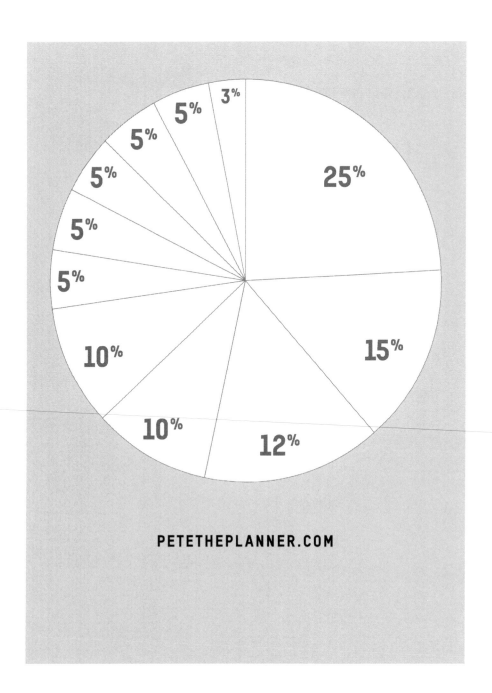

THE IDEAL HOUSEHOLD BUDGET

BUDGET CATEGORIES	RECOMMENDED PERCENTAGES	MY PERCENTAGES
Housing	25%	
Transportation	15%	
Groceries/Dining	12%	
Savings	10%	
Utilities & Phone	10%	
Charity	5%	
Entertainment	5%	
Medical	5%	
Holidays/Gifts	5%	
Clothing	5%	
Misc	3%	

25%
HOUSING

A working person can easily justify putting 25% of his or her net pay (take-home pay) toward housing. This figure doesn't include utility costs; it simply accounts for either mortgage (with taxes and insurance) or rent. Can you really justify ending your work income when one category of spending occupies such a significant part of your life? I don't think so. Consider this, if you have a net monthly household income of $4,000 prior to retirement and a $1,000 house payment, then your housing expense equals 25% of your take-home pay, as it should. But if your income dips to $3,400/month in retirement, then 29% of your income is required to make your house payment. Technically, this forces you to reduce spending in other areas of your life.

15%
TRANSPORTATION

You will find significant savings in the
transportation category in retirement.
Most retirees drive less than they did
in their working careers, and ideally,
you have eliminated your car payment.

IDEAL HOUSEHOLD BUDGET

12%
GROCERIES AND DINING

The good news during retirement is you're generally only feeding two mouths. These aren't the days of hungry teenagers with bottomless pits for stomachs. It should be pretty easy to keep your food budget at 12% of your income. And since other spending categories are greatly reduced during retirement, you may even be able to allocate more retirement income toward groceries and dining out. However, dining out too frequently is a common problem both before and during retirement. You don't want to eat your nest egg, do you? Good. Nest eggs aren't meant to be eaten.

10%
SAVINGS

During your working life, saving was vital. Theoretically, saving has allowed you to entertain these thoughts of retirement. But should you save money actively when you're retired? It depends. Don't draw more retirement income than necessary just to save money.

Distributing savings, only to re-save the money, doesn't make much sense. If you happen to receive too much income from a pension or social security and would like to save the surplus, by all means, do that. But taking a draw on your assets, just to save those assets again, is inefficient and can create some tax problems. It is worth noting many retirees do re-save money if they are forced to take withdrawals from retirement accounts. Required Minimum Distribution (RMD) rules require individuals to start taking distributions from many of their retirement accounts at age 70 ½. It's quite common for retirees to simply re-save these required distributions. Consult your tax or financial advisor to understand how RMD rules might affect you as you approach 70 ½.

IDEAL HOUSEHOLD BUDGET

10%
UTILITIES

In most cases, utility costs vary from month to month. Do everything in your power (pun intended) to make these expenses fixed costs. Many utility providers give you the opportunity to sign up for "budget billing." This program equalizes your utility expenses by taking out the seasonal fluctuations, giving you a consistent price each month. This makes a tremendous amount of sense. Any time you can take a variable expense and make it fixed, you are making budgeting easier on yourself.

5%
CHARITY

It's not unusual to see a pre-retiree's charitable contributions increase prior to and during retirement. With age comes perspective. Sensing and then acting on the needs of your community has an immeasurable impact.
You want to feel like you have enough money? Give some of it away. However, money isn't the only resource you have available as a retiree; you also have time. You can reasonably and sensibly replace your monetary contributions with volunteerism, if a monetary contribution isn't prudent.

IDEAL HOUSEHOLD BUDGET

5%
CLOTHING

Of all the expenses I see reduced in retirement, clothing is at the top of the list. It's mind-numbing to think about how much money you've spent over the course of your life on clothing. You spent money on work clothes, play clothes, church clothes, workout clothes, and going-out clothes for you, your spouse, and your children. Thankfully, you can reduce this category now.

5%
MEDICAL

This is one of the expense categories in which you can expect to spend more money than you did during your working years. According to statistics compiled from the U.S. Census Bureau, Saperston Companies, and Bankrate, the average total cost for a couple over 65 for medical treatment over a 20-year span is $215,000. Your medical expenses will be funded not only by your retirement income, but also likely by your retirement assets themselves.

IDEAL HOUSEHOLD BUDGET

5%
ENTERTAINMENT

Live. You've worked your entire life. Travel. Go to concerts. Take your sweetie to a movie. But make sure it fits into your budget. If you can objectively afford a monthly trip, take it.

5%
HOLIDAYS AND GIFTS

This category of spending is a potential problem area for most retirees. There is a dominant misconception amongst working people that retirees are wealthy. This misconception exists amongst your friends and family too, and it's dangerous, especially if you buy into it. If you have a growing family, you have more people to buy for. However, your budget, is your budget, is your budget. Don't break the bank, and risk your retirement's viability, simply because you want to buy gifts for people. Over-gifting is a serious problem, especially amongst retirees.

IDEAL HOUSEHOLD BUDGET

3%
MISCELLANEOUS

In what category do you place landscaping? Where does pet grooming go? If you happen to have expenses which fall outside the previous categories, then feel free to classify them as miscellaneous.

THE EXPENSE CATEGORIES YOU DON'T SEE

You'll notice there are a few common expense categories you don't see on the *Ideal Household Budget.* Below is a brief discussion of some of the categories left off the Ideal Household Budget.

DEBT

As we discussed earlier, debt can ruin your chance at retirement. If you have debt now, then you must carve room into your budget by significantly reducing spending in the other categories. For instance, if you are actively and aggressively trying to pay off debt, then you are likely not saving 10% of your income or giving 5% away to charity. You also shouldn't be spending 5% of your income on entertainment and 5% of your income on clothing. The best part about visualizing your budget in a pie chart is that you can then give certain categories bigger pieces of the pie when necessary. And when you have consumer debt robbing other categories of their piece of the pie, then you must rectify the situation appropriately.

LONG TERM CARE

One of the best ways to protect your retirement assets is to purchase long term care insurance. Long term care insurance, or LTC as it's commonly called, helps pay for assisted living expenses in the event your health fails. It can cost upwards of $200 per day to care for someone in a long term care facility. If you don't have protection via a long term care insurance policy, then you must use your retirement assets to pay for your care. This situation instantly becomes a problem for several reasons. Most importantly, if your income and assets are going to pay for your expensive care, then your spouse's financial needs go unanswered. Long term care insurance prevents this from happening: your assets aren't the primary source of funding for your medical expenses when you have LTC coverage. You need to have a thorough discussion with your financial advisor about how a long term care stay would affect your financial situation. Long term care insurance ranges in price, but you should budget in a few hundred dollars per month, if you purchase in your 50s. And by the way, you should purchase the policy in your 50s. It's much cheaper, the younger you are.

EDUCATION

Are you currently paying for your kids' education? Will you still be paying for the education during retirement? Let's hope not. In fact, your children's education can be one of the primary roadblocks in your retirement planning today.

BUDGETING AS A PRE-RETIREE

For many, financial success is defined as being able to afford whatever they want. However, a better definition of financial success, especially in retirement planning, is having very few financial obligations. You have finite income and assets; therefore, your ability to reduce your financial obligations allows you to stretch your economic resources further. If you want to do one thing to ensure a great retirement, learn to effectively budget as a pre-retiree.

The best way to begin budgeting as a pre-retiree is to use your bank and/or credit card statements and compile one month's worth of spending. Do your best to sort your spending into the categories we listed above. Now, compare your monthly spending to the Ideal Household Budget recommended percentages. This is the start to budgeting. By comparing what you are doing with what you should be doing, you are able to set some very simple goals.

You should look at your spending every month. We all have good months and bad months, but if you don't make adjustments for the bad months, and you don't save the extra money from the good months, then you are being incredibly inefficient. Do you think your employer knows whether or not the company had a bad month? And if so, don't you think your employer knows exactly how bad it was, from a monetary standpoint? He or she does. And you need to too. But more importantly, if you find you had a good month or even a few good months in a row, then you may be on your way to the best kept secret in the financial world.

Here's the secret: saving money is primarily good because it trains you to live on less of your available income, not because you need to accumulate money. We are on a career-long journey to wean ourselves from our incomes. Unfortunately, it often works out quite the opposite way. As we age, and as our careers progress, we tend to make more money and spend more money. We are in a constant state of upgrade. Newer house, newer car, newer clothes—newer everything. By increasing the amount of money you spend on a monthly basis as you approach retirement, you're actually moving further away from a retirement reality. The confusion comes within the perceived primary goal: accumulation. Accumulation, alone, makes for a very challenging retirement attempt. You need dual aims: accumulation and growing fiscal restraint.

For instance, let's assume you are currently saving only 10% of your income. Whereas this would be acceptable for a person or family 20 years from retirement, it's not the best situation for you. A pre-retiree, specifically someone within 10 years of retirement, should be saving much more than 10% of his or her income. It would be more appropriate to save at least 25% of your income in the last few years prior to retirement.

MAJOR PURCHASES IN RETIREMENT

Whether you realize it or not, your financial life was shaped by your major purchase decisions. You were able to save for retirement, or not save for retirement, based on how much house you purchased. In the moment, we don't really think about housing purchases in these terms. But the very first housing decision you ever made significantly impacted your retirement because our housing expense is often the largest monthly expense we have at any given point in our lives. And it doesn't stop with housing. Every major purchase decision has shaped your retirement, and always will, even when you are retired.

As we discussed earlier, you will need chunks of money in retirement to make large purchases. Sometimes these purchases are fun (trips), and sometimes these purchases are not fun (a new roof). You won't necessarily make major purchases often during retirement, but keep in mind, your margin for error is slimmer than it was when you were working. You need to be prepared to use either your chunk money for these purchases, or to set aside monthly retirement income to pay for the major purchases over time. If you choose to use income-generating assets for the purchase, you risk the ability to produce acceptable levels of future income.

In many ways, major purchases can act as a retirement roadblock if you don't properly prepare for them. But major purchases aren't the only retirement roadblocks, and they certainly aren't the sneakiest. To understand the sneakiest retirement roadblocks, you must prepare yourself for some uncomfortable truths.

CHAPTER SIX

ROADBLOCKS IN RETIREMENT

WHAT'S WORSE—BEING LIED TO WHEN THE TRUTH WOULD HURT, OR HEARING THE TRUTH THAT HURTS?

Most people claim they would much rather hear the truth. What they fail to acknowledge, however, is whether or not they will accept the truth as truth. They may listen to the truth, and then simply deny its validity. In fact, that's what most people do: it's called denial. You are about to read some very uncomfortable but important truths about retirement planning. You need to make a choice. You can either take the time to see how each of these issues affects your life, or you can simply try to discredit the veracity of these truths.

HERE ARE SOME DIFFICULT TRUTHS.

Four seemingly insignificant, yet common roadblocks can severely impact your ability to retire. Believe it or not, this doesn't include the most common, most often ignored roadblock, which is a lack of repeatable retirement income. You'd be surprised how many people assume retirement is just going to happen, despite a glaring lack of financial resources. However, the four roadblocks most people don't acknowledge are truly the most damaging.

POOR HOUSING DECISIONS

If the success of your retirement is based on your ability to balance your available income with your financial obligations, then you must start by examining what is likely your largest financial obligation: your mortgage.

If you are a homeowner, or maybe more appropriately, in the process of becoming a homeowner via a mortgage, then the reduction of this financial obligation heading into retirement is paramount to your financial success. Unfortunately, that's not a popular choice anymore. Don't confuse the issue. Pre-retirees would prefer not to have a mortgage expense in retirement, but most often their actions speak louder than their wishes. A 30-year mortgage, entered into at age 50, doesn't exactly show a commitment to being mortgage-free at retirement. Sure, there are people who greatly expedite the payoff of a 30-year mortgage in order to rid themselves of the obligation heading into retirement, yet the reality is most people who get themselves into a 30-year mortgage at age 50 have no semblance of a plan to pay it off prior to the 30-year note's maturity.

Take a moment and evaluate the role your home plays in your financial life. As a pre-retiree, does it currently cause you stress? If so, that stress is unlikely to be alleviated in retirement, unless paying off the mortgage prior to retirement is part of your plan. Ideally, you shouldn't have a mortgage payment in retirement. Sociologically, the interesting thing about this statement is three decades ago, it wouldn't have been as shocking to read. Today's financing culture has us financing things longer, and at greater amounts, than ever before. Just because mortgage lending has loosened to allow you to borrow money for housing during retirement, doesn't mean you should borrow money for housing during retirement. Even if your home is paid off in retirement, you will still have property taxes and homeowner insurance obligations every single year. Depending on a number of factors, this obligation will still cost you several thousand dollars per year.

AN UNREASONABLE HEALTHCARE STRATEGY

To say the healthcare system in the United States today is inadequate is a gross understatement. Various parts of the system create problems for people in all stages of life. As it stands now, you are eligible for Medicare when you reach age 65.

If you are currently working and your healthcare is provided through your employer, then you are most likely paying a reasonable amount of money for your health insurance coverage. And what's more, your health insurance premiums are paid by your gross income, not your net income. This means you pay your health insurance coverage well before your paycheck hits your checking account. Don't underestimate the importance of this idea. Your household budget is based on your net income (your take home pay). Many retirement plans fail to account for the cost of health insurance purchased outside of an employment agreement, if the retiree retires prior to being eligible for Medicare. You may be able to retire by every reasonable financial measure, yet be derailed by the cost of healthcare. You may have the repeatable, guaranteed income to retire. You may have cut your monthly obligations to a reasonable level. But what are you going to do when you leave your job prior to being eligible for Medicare and can't afford the $1800 month health insurance premium that comes with buying health insurance coverage on your own? Can your retirement income support another $21,600 annual expense? It's unlikely, and it's often ignored.

The solution to this problem isn't as easy as it may seem. Many pre-retirees who aren't eligible for Medicare think they can just find part-time employment that will offer them healthcare coverage. It very rarely works out that way for many reasons, one being age discrimination. Age discrimination is very sad, frustrating, and real. Whether you like it or not, it is cheaper and easier to hire a much younger worker. Look at the job you left. While your co-workers and bosses were sad about your retirement, your bosses were probably able to hire a much younger worker who costs less to pay and to insure.

You don't have a retirement strategy if you don't have a healthcare strategy. Not only that, but your healthcare strategy needs to be reasonable, achievable, and affordable. Innumerable Americans are stranded in their jobs today because of this very concept. As organizations tighten their purse strings to become economically efficient and viable, retiree healthcare options are one of the first things to be cut. These are the harsh realities of retirement in America today.

COST OF CHILDREN'S EDUCATION

Think back thirty years. Think about how parents of college students dealt with their children's educational costs. Were these obligations significant?

By most measures, no. In the last last twenty years, the cost of a college education has skyrocketed. If you have had a child attend college during this time frame, then you are undoubtedly feeling the effect of this trend in one way, shape, or form. If you have had a student pass through the halls of higher ed in the last 10 years, then chances are your student's college education has greatly impacted your retirement.

A 2013 report in the *Financial Times* suggests over 2.2 million Americans 60 and over have co-signed on private student loans for their children. If the children can't pay, then the parents are 100% responsible for the debt. Your children don't need to take out numerous student loans to get a solid education, and you certainly don't need to take out student loans to help them get a solid education. Sadly, if you make the wrong decision, you will set your retirement back years, if not a decade.

FINANCIAL SUPPORT OF ADULT CHILDREN

Prepare yourself for some discomfort. Without a doubt, one of the most damaging things you can do as you approach retirement is to financially support your adult children in any way.

Experts have called this phenomenon "failure to launch." Your inability to separate yourself from your adult child is a failure. That's what makes this situation difficult. The assertion seems both callous and unreasonable, yet cultural trends suggest this is a significant problem in our society. There are several reasons that financially assisting your adult children on a consistent basis lead to negative consequences, but ultimately you can boil it down to four major reasons.

Before we examine the four reasons why assisting your adult child is a bad idea, let's take a look at the raw data from a 2011 National Endowment for Financial Education report.

- 50% of parents supply housing to adult children who are no longer in school

- 48% of parents supply money for living expenses to adult children who are no longer in school

- 41% of parents assist with transportation costs for adult children who are no longer in school

- 35% of parents provide insurance coverage for adult children who are no longer in school

- 29% of parents occasionally front spending money for adult children who are no longer in school

- 28% of parents pay medical bills for adult children who are no longer in school

These numbers are ridiculous.

YOUR KIDS HAVE TRAINING WHEELS ON

Can you imagine the Tour de France if the cyclists rode with training wheels on their bicycles? The Tour de France is one of the most difficult athletic competitions in the world. It is very dangerous, it takes years of dedication and hard work to prepare for, and it wouldn't be possible if the athletes' parents didn't let their children fall off of their bikes.

When a child learns to ride a bike, he or she inevitably falls. A fall from a bike is usually followed by a little bit of pain and some tears. Sometimes the fall is followed by more than a little bit of pain and some tears. As a parent, it's quite difficult not only to watch your child fail, but also to watch him or her in pain. Does it make you a bad parent if your daughter falls off her bike and bloodies her knee? Absolutely not, and yet, it does take a large amount of intestinal fortitude.

Your children need to fall off of their financial bikes. They need to fail financially. It doesn't make you a bad parent if you allow your children to fail financially. It makes you a bad parent if you take away their opportunity to learn. Did they rack up a large amount of credit card debt and now can't pay their bills? It sounds like the perfect chance to learn a lesson. However, here's the very difficult part: their financial mistakes can often be attributed to you not teaching them the proper way to handle money. No one wants to read this, especially if you have been in this situation in the past.

If you have found yourself in this situation, you have to ask yourself a series of probing questions. What did you fail to teach your children about money? How can solving their problem help them learn? Did your financial assistance treat the problem, the symptoms, or the side-effects?

If you have already driven down this road of financial assistance and haven't been able to sever financial ties, then you need to before this relationship ruins your retirement. Don't think it can actually ruin, and not just damage, your retirement? It can. It can absolutely ruin it. You only have so many working years left; your child has several more working years remaining.

One of the most common manifestations of failure to launch is when a parent loans/gifts a child a down payment to purchase a home. The scenario usually goes like this: the child can afford the mortgage payment but can't qualify for the mortgage loan unless he or she has money for a down payment. The parent offers to step in and loan/gift the money for the down payment. The mortgage application is approved, and chaos ensues. What? You didn't know about the chaos part of this scenario? Let's examine the scenario from a different perspective. Why did the lending institution require a down payment? Because it's a significant measure of whether someone is a good credit risk. What did you do to the process? You destroyed it—not only for the lending institution, but also for your child. You helped your child get into a 30-year mortgage agreement he or she couldn't afford. Affording a home is more than just affording the payment. What is going to happen when the house needs a new furnace? What is going to happen if the street your child lives on needs a sewer upgrade and the homeowners on the street are responsible for paying for it? What are you going to do if your child loses his or her job?

Good parenting is helping your child avoid these situations, not facilitating them. Good parenting is letting your child get denied the loan, then showing him or her how to save the money for the down payment. Bad parenting is solving a problem that didn't exist and creating a problem that didn't exist.

BEING IN A BETTER RELATIVE POSITION, ISN'T ENOUGH

When someone asks for help, he or she generally looks for help from someone in a better financial position. When someone needs a rescue lifesaver in the water, he or she usually looks for someone who isn't in the water. When someone knocks on your door wanting to borrow a cup of sugar, he or she is simply looking for someone who has more sugar. In other words, all of these people are looking for help from someone with a relative advantage.

Just because you have more money or a higher income than another person doesn't mean you are in a position to help him or her. Human nature and parental instinct would tell you otherwise. Your unwillingness to help someone when asked can be interpreted as cruel and selfish. But it's neither. What's cruel is helping someone when you shouldn't, especially if it means hurting yourself in the process. When given pre-flight instructions on a commercial aircraft, passengers are told, in the case of an emergency, they should secure their own oxygen mask prior to assisting the person next to them. Why? Because you risk everyone's safety when you can't ensure your own safety.

DON'T IGNORE
THE ROADBLOCKS

At first glance, you may feel unaffected by these roadblocks. You need to thoroughly examine their current and future impact on your retirement, however. Your housing decision greatly impacts your income. Your healthcare costs are as big a risk to your financial future as investment risk. And it's incredibly difficult to stop parenting. The people who navigate this gauntlet of retirement roadblocks are the ones who retire comfortably and confidently.

CHAPTER SEVEN

MOCK RETIREMENT

IT'S TIME TO PRACTICE BEING RETIRED. AND NO, IT DOESN'T MEAN YOU GET TO START EATING DINNER AT 4PM.

You've just learned a tremendous amount about what retirement involves, and now it's time to put your newfound knowledge to use. You are going to retire for three months.

THIS IS YOUR MOCK RETIREMENT.

This is your opportunity to prove to yourself that retirement is not just a pipe dream. There are some rules, there is some math, and there are some circumstances to look out for along the way. The next three months won't always be easy, but the challenging moments will pale in comparison to the first three months of real retirement.

In real retirement, you don't get a second chance. In real retirement, you don't get to change your mind a few months in and go back to your old job. It generally is permanent. But permanency should not be mistaken for satisfaction. Your decisions early in the retirement process, including the years preceding retirement, will determine how you survive economically during this stage of your life. The gravity of your decisions cannot possibly be overemphasized.

Fortunately, your *Mock Retirement* is different. You get to learn on the fly, adjust on the fly, and most importantly, after the three month period, make the proper adjustments for a successful retirement. *Mock Retirement* starts now.

THE
PROCESS

Retiring while you are still working is a strange, but effective concept. It requires you to be disciplined and purposeful. You will need to measure two primary components: your projected retirement income and your projected retirement expenses. The lifeblood of your retirement is your guaranteed repeatable income. And reducing your expenses to a reasonable level will allow you to live a more comfortable retirement.

If you currently live paycheck to paycheck with very little monthly surplus, *Mock Retirement* will prove to be challenging. But this is exactly why you should be doing *Mock Retirement*. Real retirement requires tough choices, as does *Mock Retirement*. You've determined what your retirement income will be at your target retirement age. You now need to live on this monthly income for the next three months. If there is a difference in your current income and your projected retirement income, then *Mock Retirement* requires you to forego using the surplus money for lifestyle spending over the next three months. In fact, you should use this money to pay down debt, increase your retirement chunk money fund, and/or increase your income-producing retirement assets. Theoretically, if you create a surplus of $1200 per month during this process, your net worth will increase by at least $3600 over the three month period. Your net worth increase should naturally connect to debt reduction and asset accumulation. This is a good thing.

There are rare instances in which your retirement income is actually higher than your final working income. This happens for several different reasons, and *Mock Retirement* will help you determine how to deal with it. In some cases, it's because of age. When you reach a certain age, sometimes you become eligible for different income streams such as a pension or Social Security. And if you aren't currently working in the job your pension is attached to, then it's quite possible your current income is lower than the income that will be produced from the pension.

THE
CALCULATION

As you now know, you are likely to have up to four streams of income during your retirement. The more streams you have, the more diverse your income will be. The fewer streams you have, the fewer mistakes you can make in retirement planning. To review, the income streams are personal savings and investments, pension, Social Security, and (part-time) employment. You will examine each of these potential income streams, determine how much money you can expect from each, and arrive at your *Mock Retirement* income level.

First, select the hypothetical age at which you'd like to retire. This allows you to know how much income will be available for you via pension and Social Security payments. Conveniently, all Social Security statements, and most pension statements, will let you know what your monthly payment will be at different ages. For instance, your Social Security statement might indicate you have $1,600/month available at 62, and $1,800/month available at age 65. If you want to retire as soon as possible, then select the youngest age possible on both Social Security and your hypothetical pension. Additionally, you won't have regular access to your 401(k), IRAs, or a few other retirement plans, commonly referred to as qualified assets, until you reach the age of 59 ½. If a majority of your retirement assets are tied-up in qualified assets, then it will be very difficult to retire prior to 59 ½.

Don't make the mistake of setting age 60 as a retirement goal, particularly if you plan to be dependent on Social Security or pension income that might not be available until a later age. If Social Security is a key player in your retirement income story, then make sure you are projecting your retirement age to 62 at the absolute earliest.

TAXES

You cannot ignore your obligation to pay taxes—federal income taxes, state income taxes, local income taxes, capital gains taxes, and more. Don't forget there's a retirement income tax table in the Appendix of this book to help you sort through the intricacies of your particular situation. Calculating your tax obligation on your total retirement income structure is a relatively complicated process. For the purpose of *Mock Retirement*, use a 25% total tax rate. Therefore, if your retirement income streams create a gross income of $5,000 per month, then your net income will be $3,750. If you'd like a more accurate idea of your retirement tax obligations, consult your financial advisor or tax professional.

$5000 X 25% = **$1,250** $5,000 - $1,250 =**$3,750**

THE MATH

What is your current net
household income?

$$\boxed{\text{\textbf{\$}}}$$

How old are you today?

$$\boxed{}$$

Select your target
retirement age.

$$\boxed{}$$

What is the projected value of your
investments at your target retirement age?

$$\boxed{\text{\textbf{\$}}}$$

*(Need help calculating this number?
Use our calculator at PeteThePlanner.com/
Retirement-Calculator)*

How much income will your investments
produce in the first year of your retirement?

$$\boxed{}$$

*(We recommend using 4%. Multiply
your projected investment value by 4%.)*

How much Social Security income
will you have at this age?

$$\boxed{\text{\textbf{\$}}}$$

How much pension income
will you have at this age?

$$\boxed{\text{\textbf{\$}}}$$

How much part-time
employment income will
you have at this age?

$$\boxed{\text{\textbf{\$}}}$$

Total of your income streams
(gross income)

$$\boxed{\text{\textbf{\$}}}$$

Multiply by .75 *(This simulates a
25% tax rate and creates your net
monthly income.)*

$$\boxed{\text{\textbf{\$}}}$$

THE
RULES

Your mission is to live on the income you just calculated for the next three months. This may excite you, this may make you nervous, or this may terrify you. No matter how you react to the task at hand, you need to do it. Don't start searching for reasons why you can't make it happen. Instead, search for ways to make it happen. We are removing the guesswork that makes retirement planning so treacherous. By the end of your three month *Mock Retirement*, much of the guesswork will be gone. There are some rules, however.

1. Try.

2. Don't fudge the numbers to trick the system.
   You are only tricking yourself.

3. Track your progress on the budget tables at the end
   of this chapter.

4. Don't leave the manufactured surplus in your checking
   account. Get it out of there at the end of each month.

5. Take time to identify the specific spending categories you
   need to reduce in order to make Mock Retirement work.

6. Talk about your Mock Retirement openly. You don't have
   to share all the numbers with your friends and family,
   but you should be willing to talk about the concept.
   The people you tell will encourage you and hold you
   accountable to your goals. And maybe you will inspire
   them to take their retirement spending seriously too.

WHAT YOU SHOULD DO WITH YOUR MANUFACTURED SURPLUS

Most likely, you will create a monthly surplus for three months because you are limiting your spending to what your retirement income will allow you to spend. For instance, if your actual work income provides you with a total take-home pay of $6,000, but your projected retirement income only provides you with $4,800 per month, then you will have created a $1,200 monthly surplus for three months.

Your manufactured surplus has two great uses, no matter if it's large or small. The good news is both uses will increase your net worth by the same amount. Your net worth is a measure of your financial standing. It's calculated by subtracting your liabilities (debts) from your assets. If you were to use your surplus to pay down your debt by $3,600, then your net worth increases by $3,600. If you were to use your surplus to augment your savings by $3,600, then your net worth increases by $3,600. These two scenarios aren't merely examples to help you understand net worth; these two scenarios are exactly what you should do with your manufactured surplus.

You should either save the surplus, or use it to pay down debt.

Take a moment to imagine what would happen if you made your manufactured surplus permanent. What if you were able to start living on your projected retirement income right now, and you didn't stop living on it until retirement? How would your retirement transition feel? Would you have confidence in your ability to retire? Would you be able to greatly increase your net worth over this time frame? If you want to take this concept to the next level, call your financial advisor and commit your manufactured surplus to a monthly investment plan. Then again, if you have consumer debt, wipe that out first.

Earlier in the book, we discussed that 80% of 30-54 year olds don't believe they will have enough money to retire. Unfortunately, this is because they are guessing. You can stop guessing by making ends meet. If you commit to a lifestyle change spurred by your *Mock Retirement*, then you will ensure your income needs actually meet your retirement income. You are the determining factor when it comes to success; luck is not.

YOUR MOCK
RETIREMENT INCOME $ [_____]

HOUSING		TRANSPORTATION	
Mortgage/Rent		Car Payment A	
Electric		Car Payment B	
Gas		Gasoline	
Phone		Maintenance	
Cell		Auto Insurance	
Cable		License Plates	
Internet		**TOTAL**	
Water			
Waste		**FOOD**	
Lawncare		Groceries	
HOA		Coffee	
Other		Work Lunch	
TOTAL		Dining Out	
		TOTAL	

PERSONAL CARE		EXISTING DEBT	
Clothing		Debt Payment #1	
Cleaning/Laundry		Debt Payment #2	
Hair Care		Debt Payment #3	
Medical		Debt Payment #4	
Books/Subscriptions		Debt Payment #5	
Entertainment		Debt Payment #6	
Gifts		Debt Payment #7	
Pets		Debt Payment #8	
TOTAL		**TOTAL**	

SAVINGS AND INSURANCE

Savings	
Life/LTC Insurance	
IRA/Roth IRA	
College Savings	
TOTAL	

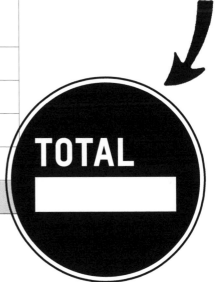

TOTAL

YOUR MOCK
RETIREMENT INCOME $ [   ]

HOUSING

		TRANSPORTATION	
Mortgage/Rent		Car Payment A	
Electric		Car Payment B	
Gas		Gasoline	
Phone		Maintenance	
Cell		Auto Insurance	
Cable		License Plates	
Internet		**TOTAL**	
Water			
Waste		**FOOD**	
Lawncare		Groceries	
HOA		Coffee	
Other		Work Lunch	
TOTAL		Dining Out	
		TOTAL	

MOCK RETIREMENT

Month two

PERSONAL CARE			EXISTING DEBT	
Clothing			Debt Payment #1	
Cleaning/Laundry			Debt Payment #2	
Hair Care			Debt Payment #3	
Medical			Debt Payment #4	
Books/Subscriptions			Debt Payment #5	
Entertainment			Debt Payment #6	
Gifts			Debt Payment #7	
Pets			Debt Payment #8	
TOTAL			**TOTAL**	

SAVINGS AND INSURANCE		
Savings		
Life/LTC Insurance		
IRA/Roth IRA		
College Savings		
TOTAL		

TOTAL

YOUR MOCK
RETIREMENT INCOME $ [   ]

HOUSING

Mortgage/Rent	
Electric	
Gas	
Phone	
Cell	
Cable	
Internet	
Water	
Waste	
Lawncare	
HOA	
Other	
TOTAL	

TRANSPORTATION

Car Payment A	
Car Payment B	
Gasoline	
Maintenance	
Auto Insurance	
License Plates	
TOTAL	

FOOD

Groceries	
Coffee	
Work Lunch	
Dining Out	
TOTAL	

MOCK RETIREMENT

Month three

PERSONAL CARE		EXISTING DEBT	
Clothing		Debt Payment #1	
Cleaning/Laundry		Debt Payment #2	
Hair Care		Debt Payment #3	
Medical		Debt Payment #4	
Books/Subscriptions		Debt Payment #5	
Entertainment		Debt Payment #6	
Gifts		Debt Payment #7	
Pets		Debt Payment #8	
TOTAL		**TOTAL**	

SAVINGS AND INSURANCE	
Savings	
Life/LTC Insurance	
IRA/Roth IRA	
College Savings	
TOTAL	

TOTAL

CHAPTER EIGHT

PLAN. ADJUST. REPEAT.

PLAN. ADJUST. REPEAT.

Upon completing your *Mock Retirement,* you will have a tremendous amount of information about your financial life and future. You may learn you've got some work to do, on both sides of the ledger. Remember, you can attack retirement from both sides. You can reduce your dependency on your current income by paying down consumer debt, saving, or investing your money. *Mock Retirement* is incredibly efficient for this very reason.

Ignoring your findings would be a horrendous mistake. It's one thing to proceed toward retirement guessing everything will be fine, it's a whole different beast to proceed toward retirement knowing your plan doesn't work. It's arguable you will never have a better grasp on your financial reality than you will upon finishing *Mock Retirement*. You can't waste that opportunity.

If you have a great amount of work left to do in order to create a viable retirement plan, then you need to take immediate action. You can't view your financial changes as a diet. This is not a diet. People who make sudden, trendy health changes rarely make the changes stick. A person achieves true health when he or she decides to start living healthy, permanently. And likewise, grasping success out of the jaws of defeat requires a permanent financial lifestyle change. Again, your spending changes will feed your ability to accumulate assets, pay down debt, and lose your dependency to your income. Once you've made some changes, let some time pass (12-18 months), and then do another *Mock Retirement*. There is absolutely no reason why you shouldn't do a *Mock Retirement* until you get it right. Otherwise, you are just guessing. Unfortunately, guessing and retirement planning are a terrible combination.

WHAT A SUCCESSFUL MOCK RETIREMENT INDICATES

It is entirely possible you have a giant smile on your face right now because your *Mock Retirement* went very well. You saw how your projected retirement income coordinated with your projected retirement expenses. If this is the case, your work still isn't done. The *Mock Retirement* exercise is filled with variables. We made several assumptions along the way. Your job now is to make sure these assumptions come to fruition. Did you assume you were earning a 7% rate of return on your investments? If so, you sure better get a 7% rate of return. Not only must you get that return, but you also must take the least amount of risk possible to get the job done. There is no reason to expose your retirement plan to unnecessary risk.

Suppose I were to tell you that, hypothetically, you just need a 3% rate of return on your investments to accomplish all of your retirement goals. Should you try to get more than a 3% rate of return? In order to get a higher rate of return, typically you must take more risk. When you take more risk, you increase your chances of having your money shrink. You don't want your money to shrink. I believe you should take just enough risk to get the job done. In fact, this is exactly why you should discuss your risk and investment plans with an investment advisor.

THE IMPORTANCE OF A RELATIONSHIP WITH A FINANCIAL ADVISOR

You undoubtedly can sense how I feel about the importance of having a great financial advisor. A financial advisor should bring knowledge, experience, and accountability to the table. He or she should be able to help you come to terms with your risk tolerance, asset allocation, and distribution rate. You will be able to get the detailed answers to your specific tax situation, and you will be able to further discuss pension and Social Security options.

If you are a do-it-yourselfer, please take the time to fully understand distribution rates, investment time horizon, and all risks, including, but not limited to, market risk. It's very hard, if not impossible, to reverse some retirement decisions if you happen to make a mistake. It makes sense to get a second set of eyes to look over your retirement plan if you did it completely by yourself. There's no room for pride in a decision this significant.

YOUR FINANCIAL BEHAVIOR MUST MATCH YOUR GOAL

As you continue on your path toward retiring, visit *PeteThePlanner.com* frequently for free resources, encouragement, and instruction. You must stay engaged in the process. If you want to be able to relax during retirement, then you must do everything in your power to make sure your plan actually works. Just think, by the time you get to retirement, you will have already retired once, and you'll know you can do it.

A simple 12-page companion workbook for Mock Retirement is available at *PeteThePlanner.com/PeteMart.*

APPENDIX

Retirement Inc. Sources Table

Income Sources and Tax Implications

SOCIAL SECURITY

TAX IMPLICATIONS

- If the only income you received during the tax year was your Social Security or equivalent railroad retirement benefits, your benefits may not be taxable and you may not have to file a tax return.[1]
- If you also received other income, your benefits will not be taxable unless your modified adjusted gross income (MAGI) is more than the base amount for your filing status. If you have income in addition to your benefits, you may have to file a return even if none of your benefits are taxable. [2]
- The taxable benefits, if any, must be included in the gross income of the person who has the legal right to receive them. If you are married and file a joint return, you and your spouse must combine your incomes, social security benefits, and equivalent railroad retirement benefits when figuring the taxable portion of your benefits. Even if your spouse did not receive any benefits, you must add your spouse's income to yours when figuring if any of your benefits are taxable, if you file a joint return. [3]

- No one pays federal income tax on more than 85 percent of his or her Social Security benefits based on Internal Revenue Service (IRS) rules. If you:

  - File a federal tax return as an "individual" and your combined income is:
    —between $25,000 and $34,000, you may have to pay income tax on up to 50 percent of your benefits.
    —more than $34,000, up to 85 percent of your benefits may be taxable.

  - File a joint return, and you and your spouse have a combined income that is between $32,000 and $44,000, you may have to pay income tax on up to 50 percent of your benefits
    —more than $44,000, up to 85 percent of your benefits may be taxable.

  - Are married and file a separate tax return, you probably will pay taxes on your benefits.[4]

1   http://www.irs.gov/taxtopics/tc423.html
2   http://www.irs.gov/taxtopics/tc423.html
3   http://www.irs.gov/taxtopics/tc423.html
4   http://www.socialsecurity.gov/planners/taxes.htm

PENSION PAYMENTS

- If you receive pension or annuity payments before age 59 ½, you may be subject to an additional 10% tax on early distributions unless the distribution qualifies for an exemption. The additional tax does not apply to any part of a distribution that is tax free or to any of the following types of distributions:
    - Distributions made as a part of a series of substantially equal periodic payments from a qualified plan that begins after your separation from service
    - Distributions made because you are totally and permanently disabled
    - Distributions made on or after the death of the plan participant or contract holder, and
    - Distributions made from a qualified retirement plan after your separation from service and in or after the year you reached age 55[5]

- The pension or annuity payments that you receive are fully taxable if you have no investment in the contract because any of the following situations apply:
    - The pension or annuity payments that you receive are fully taxable if you have no investment in the contract because any of the following situations apply:
    - You did not contribute anything or are not considered to have contributed anything for the pension or annuity
    - Your employer did not withhold contributions from your salary, or
    - You received all of your contributions (your investment in the contract) tax free in prior years[6]

- If you contributed after-tax dollars to your pension or annuity, your pension payments are partially taxable. You will not pay tax on the part of the payment that represents a return of the after-tax amount you paid. This amount is your investment in the contract, and includes the amounts your employer contributed that were taxable to you when contributed.[7]

5   http://www.irs.gov/taxtopics/tc410.html

6   http://www.irs.gov/taxtopics/tc410.html

7   http://www.irs.gov/taxtopics/tc410.html

PENSION LUMP-SUM

- If the lump-sum distribution qualifies, you can elect to treat the portion of the payment attributable to your active participation in the plan using one of five options:
  - Report the part of the distribution from participation before 1974 as a capital gain (if you qualify) and the part of the distribution from participation after 1973 as ordinary income.
  - Report the part of the distribution from participation before 1974 as a capital gain (if you qualify) and use the 10-year tax option to figure the tax on the part from participation after 1973 (if you qualify).
  - Use the 10-year tax option to figure the tax on the total taxable amount (if you qualify).
  - Roll over all or part of the distribution. No tax is currently due on the part rolled over. Report any part not rolled over as ordinary income.
  - Report the entire taxable part as ordinary income.[8]

401K

- If you withdraw money from a qualified retirement plan, you may be subject to an additional tax of 10%. This is penalty for taking an early distribution from an individual retirement account (IRA), 401(k), 403(b), or other qualified retirement plan before reaching age **59½**.[9]
- There are exceptions to the additional 10% tax; they can be found under IRS Tax Topic 558.[10]
- Distributions from your 401(k) plan are taxable unless the amounts are rolled over.[11]

9   http://www.irs.gov/taxtopics/tc558.html
10   http://www.irs.gov/taxtopics/tc558.html
11   http://www.irs.gov/Retirement-Plans/Plan-Participant,-Employee/401(k)-Resource-Guide---Plan-Participants---General-Distribution-Rules

ROTH IRA (INDIVIDUAL RETIREMENT ACCOUNT)

TAX IMPLICATIONS

- If you satisfy the requirements, qualified distributions are tax-free. [12]
- If you receive a distribution that is not a qualified distribution, you may have to pay the 10% additional tax on early distributions. [13]
- You may not have to pay the 10% additional tax in the following situations. [14]
  - You have reached age 59½.
  - You are totally and permanently disabled.
  - You are the beneficiary of a deceased IRA owner.
  - You use the distribution to buy, build, or rebuild a first home.
  - The distributions are part of a series of substantially equal payments.
  - You have unreimbursed medical expenses that are more than 7.5% of your adjusted gross income.
  - You are paying medical insurance premiums during a period of unemployment.
  - The distributions are not more than your qualified higher education expenses.
  - The distribution is due to an IRS levy of the qualified plan.
  - The distribution is a qualified reservist distribution.

- Contributions to a Roth IRA are not deductible (and you do not report the contributions on your tax return), but you also are not taxed on qualified distributions or distributions that are a return of contributions. In addition, you do not have to be under age 70½ to contribute to a Roth IRA. To be a Roth IRA, the account or annuity must be designated as a Roth IRA when it is set up[15]

12 http://www.irs.gov/publications/p590/index.html
13 http://www.irs.gov/publications/p590/index.html
14 http://www.irs.gov/publications/p590/index.html
15 http://www.irs.gov/taxtopics/tc451.html

IRA (INDIVIDUAL RETIREMENT ACCOUNT)

TAX IMPLICATIONS

- Distributions from a traditional IRA are fully or partially taxable in the year of distribution. If you made only deductible contributions, distributions are fully taxable. Use Form 8606 to figure the taxable portion of withdrawals.[16]
- Distributions made prior to age 59½ may be subject to a 10% additional tax. You also may owe an excise tax if you do not begin to withdraw minimum distributions by April 1st of the year after you reach age 70½.[17]
- If you withdraw money from a **SIMPLE IRA** and you first began participating in a SIMPLE IRA plan within the past two years, then your early distribution penalty is **25%** instead of 10%.[18]
- There are exceptions that can be found under IRS Tax Topic 558.[19]
- Contributions to a traditional IRA might be fully deductible, partially deductible or entirely nondeductible, depending on various factors.[20]

16 http://www.irs.gov/taxtopics/tc451.html
17 http://www.irs.gov/taxtopics/tc451.html
18 http://www.irs.gov/Retirement-Plans/Plan-Participant,-Employee/
    Retirement-Topics---Tax-on-Early-Distributions
19 http://www.irs.gov/taxtopics/tc558.html
20 http://www.irs.gov/publications/p590/ch01.html#en_US_2012_
    publink1000230394

RENT - LANDLORD

TAX IMPLICATIONS

- You generally must include in your gross income all amounts you receive as rent. Rental income is any payment you receive for the use or occupation of property.[21]
- Expenses of renting property can be deducted from your gross rental income. You generally deduct your rental expenses in the year you pay them.[22]
- If your tenant pays any of your expenses, the payments are rental income. You must include them in your income.[23]
- If you have any personal use of a vacation home or other dwelling unit that you rent out, you must divide your expenses between rental use and personal use. [24]

21 http://www.irs.gov/Businesses/Small-Businesses-&-Self-Employed/Rental-Income-and-Expenses---Real-Estate-Tax-Tips
22 http://www.irs.gov/Businesses/Small-Businesses-&-Self-Employed/Rental-Income-and-Expenses---Real-Estate-Tax-Tips
23 http://www.irs.gov/Businesses/Small-Businesses-&-Self-Employed/Rental-Income-and-Expenses---Real-Estate-Tax-Tips
24 http://www.irs.gov/Businesses/Small-Businesses-&-Self-Employed/Rental-Income-and-Expenses---Real-Estate-Tax-Tips

ANNUITY PAYMENTS

TAX IMPLICATIONS

- The pension or annuity payments that you receive are fully taxable if you have no investment in the contract because any of the following situations apply:[25]
  - You did not contribute anything or are not considered to have contributed anything for the pension or annuity
  - Your employer did not withhold contributions from your salary, or
  - You received all of your contributions (your investment in the contract) tax free in prior years

- If the starting date of your pension or annuity payments is after November 18, 1996, you generally must use the Simplified Method to determine how much of your annuity payments are taxable and how much is tax free.[26]
- If you receive pension or annuity payments before age 59 ½, you may be subject to an additional 10% tax on early distributions unless the distribution qualifies for an exemption.[27]

25 http://www.irs.gov/taxtopics/tc410.html
26 http://www.irs.gov/taxtopics/tc410.html
27 http://www.irs.gov/taxtopics/tc410.html

IRA (INDIVIDUAL RETIREMENT ACCOUNT)

TAX IMPLICATIONS

- If you withdraw funds before your annuity starting date and your annuity is under a qualified retirement plan, a ratable part of the amount withdrawn is tax free. The tax-free part is based on the ratio of your cost (investment in the contract) to your account balance under the plan.[28]
- If you withdraw funds (other than as an annuity) on or after your annuity starting date, the entire amount withdrawn is generally taxable.[29]
- The amount you receive in a full surrender of your annuity contract at any time is tax free to the extent of any cost that you have not previously recovered tax free. The rest is taxable.[30]

28 http://www.irs.gov/publications/p575/ar02.html#en_US_2012_publink1000226685
29 http://www.irs.gov/publications/p575/ar02.html#en_US_2012_publink1000226685
30 http://www.irs.gov/publications/p575/ar02.html#en_US_2012_publink1000226685

Consult with your tax advisor or your financial advisor to learn more about your particular tax situation.

ACKNOWLEDGMENTS

The writing process is never about the author. This book wouldn't have been possible without the support and help of hundreds, if not thousands, of people. From past clients who were the early guinea pigs for *Mock Retirement* to radio listeners and blog readers, everyone's feedback has been vital.

My study of financial habits would not be possible without the support and work of my co-worker and right hand wo-man, Beth Weingart. She is the glue that holds things together.

Special thanks to my research assistant Alex Eaton, who helped with statistical research. Also, thanks to a tremendous number of other people for their support as well: CJ McClanahan, Lindsay Hadley, Tim Lisko, Sarah Dunn, Roy Lederman, Doug Rotman, Terry Cox, Jim Wolf, T. Ray Phillips, Mike and Conni Dunn, Ollie, Ted, WIBC, Emmis Communications, Tribune Broadcasting, Fox 59, Gannett, *The Indianapolis Star*, Raquel Richardson, Brian Smith, Charlie Morgan, Rich Jones, Michelle Payne, Todd Shickel, Ross Graham, and Marc Williams.

ABOUT THE AUTHOR

Peter Dunn a.k.a. Pete the Planner is a personal finance expert, radio host, and author. He released his first book, *What Your Dad Never Taught You About Budgeting*, in 2006 and is the host of the popular radio show The Pete the Planner Radio Show. Peter has appeared regularly on Fox News, Fox Business, CNN Headline News and numerous nationally syndicated radio programs.

His second book, *60 Days to Change: A Daily How To Guide With Actionable Tips to Improve Your Financial Life*, was released in December of 2009. His third book, *Avoid Student Loans*, was released in January 2012. Peter released the second edition of *What Your Dad Never Taught You About Budgeting* in July 2012.

Peter has been in the financial industry since 1998 and owned a financial planning practice for nearly 13 years. His primary focus since 2008 has been financial wellness in the workplace. He lists some of the largest organizations in the world as clients. His financial wellness curriculum encourages people come to terms with their money habits and helps them put together practical solutions to reduce financial stress. Peter is an expert speaker who works with organizations nationwide to motivate and excite the audience about financial wellness.

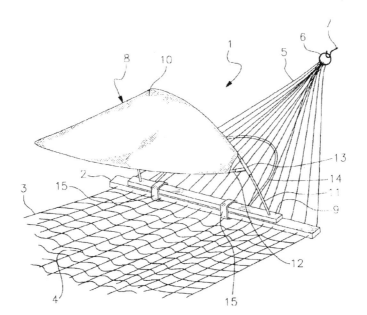